Indian Philosophy

Raghavan Srinivasan is a chemical engineer (Madras University) and an MBA from McMaster University, Canada. He currently works as a development professional and has written a number of articles for print and online newspapers as well as international journals. He co-edits an online magazine called *Ghadar Jari Hai*. Raghavan is passionate about various aspects of Indian history and writes regularly on the same. His published books include *Rajaraja Chola*, *Yugantar*, *Dogged Pursuit* and *Indian Cities*.

Quick and Concise

INDIAN PHILOSOPHY

Raghavan Srinivasan

hachette INDIA

First published in 2024 by Hachette India
(Registered name: Hachette Book Publishing India Pvt. Ltd)
An Hachette UK company
www.hachetteindia.com

The copyright details and credits for the photographs in the book are on page 195

ISBN 978-93-5731-899-0

Hachette Book Publishing India Pvt. Ltd
4th/5th Floors, Corporate Centre,
Plot No. 94, Sector 44, Gurugram 122003, India

Typeset in Cambria 10.5/12.6 by Preeti Gupta

Printed and bound in India
by Manipal Technologies Limited

MIX
Paper | Supporting responsible forestry
FSC www.fsc.org FSC™ C043100

To those great sages, seers and commentators who devoted their lives to the quest for truth and the discovery of the spiritual and philosophical essence of man.

Contents

Table of Figures

Preface

The foundations of Indian culture are deeply rooted in its rich philosophical heritage, which has been the guiding light amidst the diverse facets of art, architecture, literature, religion and more. This heritage has transcended the ages, and remained steadfast against the tides of political changes and foreign invasions. As India stands perplexed in front of the rising tide of divisiveness, it is crucial to delve into the essence of its philosophical roots.

The unfolding chapters of Indian philosophy reveal not only a historical narrative but also a discourse that resonates with timeless enquiries and solutions, still pertinent in today's philosophical debates. Exploring the annals of Indian philosophical thought opens a doorway to understanding and appreciating the essence of Indian culture, untainted by misconceptions. The interplay of various philosophical systems offers a profound insight into the evolution of thought and the potential wisdom it carries for modern intellectual pursuits.

To truly grasp the essence of Indian thought, it is imperative to revisit the wisdom of bygone eras while considering the context in which they originated and aligning them with contemporary intellectual and spiritual aspirations. While caution is warranted against superimposing present-day interpretations on historical terms, it is essential to acknowledge the timeless relevance of certain perennial issues. Delving into our past reveals both shortcomings and strengths. To draw inspiration from history, we must approach it with discernment and empathy. The pinnacles of human intellect and spirit are not confined to yesteryears; the path to the future is boundless and beckoning.

With a focus on exploring the inner philosophical realms of various systems, this work aspires to be a guiding beacon for scholars, lay readers intrigued by philosophy, and students seeking to comprehend the profound wisdom enshrined in the annals of Indian thought.

1

Exploring the Depths of Indian Philosophical Insight

The term *philosophy* is etymologically derived from a Greek word meaning 'love of knowledge'. However, an analysis of the Indian term *darshana* might provide more pertinent insights. *Darshana* encompasses a comprehensive notion beyond the conventional understanding of philosophy. It denotes a profound 'view' or 'vision' that transcends mere intellectual contemplation, embodying a holistic way of seeing and understanding the world. *Darshana* encompasses not only theoretical propositions but also practical insights, spiritual perspectives and ethical considerations, reflecting a rich tradition of experiential wisdom and critical reflection on the nature of reality, human existence and cosmic order. In Indian philosophical discourse, *darshana* serves as a lens through which profound truths are elucidated, guiding individuals on the path to self-realization, metaphysical understanding and ethical conduct.

Throughout the history of civilizations, some fundamental questions have intrigued the human mind, such as the origins of the universe, humanity's relationship with nature and the quest for the ultimate truth that can illuminate our future.

> **The pursuit of self-understanding, epitomized by the question, *Who am I?* was central to ancient Indian and classical philosophy.**

Indian philosophical traditions have long emphasized the possibility of a direct realization of truth (*tattvadarshana*), positing that those who attain such insight experience liberation, while those without it remain entangled in worldly attachments.

Contrasting with the categorization of modern Western philosophy into metaphysics, epistemology,[1] logic,[2] ethics,[3] aesthetics,[4] political philosophy[5] and axiology,[6] Indian philosophy takes a more syncretic approach, intertwining these areas of enquiry rather than treating them as discrete compartments. Furthermore, Indian philosophical enquiry methods and the evolution of philosophical thought differ significantly from those of Western philosophy, showcasing a holistic and distinct approach rooted in the darshanic tradition.

Indian philosophy, represented by a diverse array of schools or *darshanas*, encompasses a spectrum of philosophical ideologies – ranging from idealistic to materialistic, theistic to atheistic. The works of renowned philosophers like Ramanuja and Madhava, who belonged to a specific religious sect, manifested this diversity. Madhava, in his seminal work, *Sarva-Darsana-Sangraha*, canvassed a broad spectrum of views, including those of unorthodox schools like Buddhism, Jainism, and the Charvakas, alongside orthodox schools. This intricate web of diversity underscores the expansive and inclusive nature of Indian philosophical thought.

A distinctive feature of Indian philosophy lies in its broad-minded quest for truth. While philosophers of various schools espoused divergent perspectives and conclusions, they adhered to a methodology that involved understanding and engaging deeply with the viewpoints of other schools before presenting their own arguments. This dialectical process involved articulating the opponent's position (*poorvapaksha*), rigorously challenging it point by point (*khandana*) and finally putting forth their own perspective (*uttarapaksha*).

2

Harappan Civilization: Exploring Ancient Insights and Beliefs

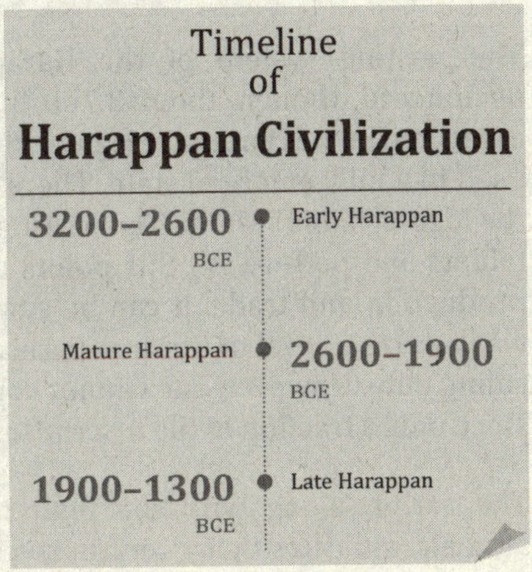

It was also thought that the Harappan civilization was predominantly an urban one, but recent discoveries have thrown up several large rural sites in addition to many cities and towns spread over a huge area. Although the Harappan sites have many common features, there are also significant differences between cities, towns and villages and also different geographical locations. Though they were connected by trade routes and seem to have followed common standards of weights, construction and planning, many variances have been noticed concerning the occupations, crops grown, social customs, cult-like practices and funerary and ritual practices.

Going by the materialist outlook that philosophy at a given period must correspond to the prevailing economic base, one can come to well-substantiated conclusions. Initially, the Harappan civilization was thought to have been greatly influenced by the Mesopotamian civilization. However, scholars have concluded that the Harappan civilization evolved independently and had its own economy and polity.

The fact that cities and towns were well-developed point to a comfortable surplus from agricultural activities and a subsistence base that supported the urban and semi-urban economy. All these indicate a certain level of economic and social development over which statecraft, culture and philosophy could flourish.

The writing system of the Harappans has still not been deciphered, though about 3,700 inscribed objects have been excavated in the Harappan region. The script seems to have been used in a fully emerged state. There are 400–500 basic signs in the logo-syllabic system. The writing appears on seals, sealings, tablets and pottery. All this points to the use of script in craft production and trade. It can be surmised from this that there was a certain level of literacy, perhaps limited to cities and the ruling elite. However, one cannot come to a definite conclusion since only a fraction of the inscriptions have survived over time.

The script, along with the figures of gods, goddesses and animals, indicates that a certain level of culture and philosophy must have been achieved in the civilization. One of the major hallmarks of the Harappan civilization is the worship of female goddesses and the association of rituals with fertility. This is in line with the preoccupation of agricultural societies around the world with fertility. A large number of terracotta female figurines have been discovered, which are generally associated with mother goddesses. There are also many female figurines that were broken, and therefore, could have been votive offerings and not images of goddesses. The figure of a male god with a buffalo-horn headdress, seated on a dais with legs bent, has been named Pashupati, the god of animals, since he is flanked by many animals. Some scholars have noticed a resemblance between this figure and the deity Shiva in later Hindu worship. Various seals depicting animals and composite animals may have religious significance. There is also evidence of animal sacrifice during rituals.

The Mother Goddess

The philosophical implications of all this evidence are complex. The mature Harappan phase lasted for at least 700 years, indicating a stable political structure, and hence, a developed culture and philosophy.

The relative absence of war implements suggests that the Harappans were a peaceful people.

The large number of female figurines and the fact that it was an agricultural society suggests that women had an important role in society, though it cannot be ascertained for sure. The absence of large monuments, supreme gods and priest-kings may point to a tribal society organized on the lines of kinship but also displays a level of state development. In comparison to the civilizations of Egypt and Mesopotamia, the absence of the paraphernalia of the elite, such as royal tombs, palaces and temples, may lead us to the conclusion that it was a relatively egalitarian society. This is further confirmed by the distribution of artefacts in all sections of the urban and rural habitations and the large differences in the size of dwellings.

***Figure 1:** Mother goddess statue wearing ornate necklace, Mohenjo-Daro, Pakistan*

Based on the agricultural nature of the Harappan civilization and the large number of female figurines, some scholars have associated it with mother goddesses and a matriarchal society, characteristic of early agricultural societies. They have also argued on differences in philosophical outlook between the pre-Aryan civilizations and the Aryan civilization, which was predominantly pastoral in its early stages. They have drawn parallels between the mother goddesses of this civilization and the later cult of Shaktism and the existence of a huge number of female *gramadevatas*, village deities in India till today. They have also speculated on the continuance of the Harappan philosophy in tribal societies of India that have survived till today and the great veneration that female deities such as Durga, Kali and Chandi command in the rural parts of India among peasants.

Key Takeaways

- The Harappan civilization, with its diverse cities, towns and villages, showcased variations in occupation, social customs and ritual practices.
- Agriculture was the primary occupation, supporting well-developed urban economies and enabling cultural and philosophical growth.
- Harappan artefacts, such as seals, copper, gold and bronze figurines, reflect a high level of craftsmanship and economic sophistication.
- The Harappan script, though undeciphered, suggests literacy and potential trade activity.
- The worship of female goddesses and fertility rituals indicate a developed cultural and philosophical milieu.
- The absence of significant war-related artefacts and the prevalence of female figurines hint at a peaceful and possibly egalitarian society.
- The association of Harappan civilization with mother goddesses and matriarchal society has drawn comparisons to later religious beliefs in India, such as Shaktism.

Fact Check (Answers at the back)

1. What was the primary occupation of the Harappan civilization? A) Animal husbandry B) Agriculture C) Foraging D) Trading
2. What does the presence of seals and copper and bronze figurines suggest about the Harappan civilization? A) Limited technological advancement B) Lack of trade networks C) High level of craftsmanship D) Minimal economic activity
3. Which of the following statements is true about the Harappan script? A) It has been fully deciphered. B) It was primarily used for religious texts. C) Evidence suggests a high level of literacy. D) It was exclusively employed in administrative tasks.
4. What religious practices were associated with the worship of female figurines in the Harappan civilization? A) Animal sacrifice B) Rituals of purification C) Fertility rituals D) Worship of warrior deities
5. What societal characteristics have some scholars associated with the Harappan civilization? A) Patriarchal society B) Egalitarian society C) Warrior society D) Caste-based society

3

The Vedas: Tribal and Pastoral Origins

Timeline of the Samhitas

1500–1100 BCE — Rig Veda

Sama Veda — 1200–800 BCE

1100–800 BCE — Yajur Veda

Atharva Veda — 1000–800 BCE

During the period 1500–600 BCE, besides archaeological evidence, we can also rely on the Vedic texts to understand the life of the people and their culture and philosophy. This period covers the early Vedic period (1500–1100 BCE) in the Bronze Age and the later Vedic period (1100–600 BCE) in the Iron Age.

We find a big transition in this period. The earlier Indus Valley Civilization, which flourished in cities, towns and villages, had given way to the Vedic civilization, which was basically pastoral. In a way, it was a setback in terms of economic advancement, a degradation from an urban, agricultural and trading economy to a pastoral, clan-led economy. Since written texts from the Indus Valley Civilization have not been deciphered, a thorough comparison of the philosophical outlook of the two civilizations is not possible, though we can certainly say that they would have differed enormously.

Among the Vedic corpus, the Samhitas, or the collection of verses, are the earliest. They consist of the Rig Veda, Sama Veda, Yajur Veda and Atharva Veda. Of these, the Rig Veda is the earliest. The Sama Veda consists of stanzas taken mostly from the Rig Veda. Hence, it has no independent philosophical value. The Yajur Veda also contains verses from the Rig Veda, but in addition, it has many original verses. The Atharva Veda is not only entirely different from the Rig Veda but represents a more primitive stage of thought in that it is a book of spells and incantations appealing to the demon world.

The earliest sections of the Rig Veda were composed between 1500 and 1000 BCE. It is possible that parts of the Rig Veda were composed even earlier since there was a tradition of transmitting the verses verbally from generation to generation until they were written using a script. The verses in the Rig Veda were all not composed at the same time. Scholars have been able to identify layers and also classify verses as earlier and later ones based on their style and the meaning of the verses. The geographical area in which they were composed includes eastern Afghanistan and Punjab, basically the area ruled by the Kuru–Panchala clans in the upper Ganga valley.

The dominant view among scholars today is that the Indo-Aryans migrated into the Indian subcontinent from the plains of Eastern Europe. The idea, promoted particularly during colonial times, that the Aryans invaded the subcontinent and drove away the indigenous people has been debunked. There were several waves of Indo-Aryan migrations. There were also cultural and language differences between these waves. The use of the horse and chariot may have given the Aryans more mobility and political power.

The Vedic Society

The Rig Veda is the product of a tribal and pastoral civilization. The verses mention thirty clans and tribes, of which the most prominent are the Purus and the Bharatas. Rig Vedic hymns refer to wars and conflicts. Many hymns express the wish of the reciter to achieve victory over their enemies, called Dasa and Dasyus. The Rig Veda also has many non-Aryan words, indicating that the Aryans had connections with people speaking Dravidian and Munda languages. The text also refers to conflicts within the Aryans, such as the 'battle of ten kings' waged by the Bharata chief Sudas against a confederacy of ten tribes.

> **The Rig Veda**
>
> The Rig Veda is the oldest known text written in Sanskrit. It is one of the four Vedas constituting the *Samhitas*. Not all of it was written in one period. Moreover, before being captured in text, the hymns of the Rig Veda were transmitted orally, possibly from the second half of the second millennium BCE. The people who composed the hymns lived in the north-western region of the Indian subcontinent.
>
> The Rig Veda is a collection of ten books called the mandalas. It has 1,028 hymns (*sukthas*) containing 10,600 verses. Not all the ten books were composed at the same time. Books 2–9 seem to be the earliest and describe deities, rites and rituals. Books 1 and 10 appear to be the more recent ones. They deal with philosophical and speculative questions. There are enquiries about the origins of the universe and the relationship of man to nature.

The Vedic state was by no means a full-fledged monarchical state. The word *rajan* mentioned in the verses can be surmised as a tribal chieftain. The Rig Vedic verses describe a seven-part state headed by the *rajan*, who is elected based on leadership qualities. Assemblies such as the *sabha* and the *samiti* conducted the daily affairs of the tribe. The *sabha* was a committee of the elite or elders in the tribe. The *samiti* was a larger assembly, presumably comprising the adult members of the society, presided by the rajan. The *vidatha* was a congregation of citizens to perform socio-religious rituals for the well-being of the tribe or clan. This stage can be called the stage of primitive communism, when class differentiation had not yet set in and all members of the society had a role to play in the daily affairs of life.

The predominant economy was pastoral while there is evidence that agriculture also played an important secondary role.

Income from these enterprises was supplemented by plunder and loot from other tribes. The concept of individual private property, as we know it today, did not exist in those times. The entire clan shared resources such as land, cattle and water sources. At the same time, not all members were equal. There is no evidence of wage labour in the sense of an owner of means of production paying wages for work. But there is mention of slavery, in which the slaves had no power and rights in society. As in other civilizations, the enslavement of women would have been far more brutal, including sexual exploitation, compared to the enslavement of men. The Vedic people consumed milk and ate fruits, vegetables and grains. They were also meat eaters. There are references related to the sacrificial offering of sheep, goats and oxen. There are references to the cow as *aghnya* (not to be killed), but this is not to be confused with the issue of the religious sanctity of the cow as we experience it today.

There is a lot of manufacturing activity mentioned in the hymns, such as carpentry, metal works, chariot making, agricultural implements, weaving and other occupations. It is possible that some households or groups of members engaged in specialized full-time crafts and manufacturing. The Rig Vedic people engaged in barter. There is mention of roads and chariots used to transport goods and trade though the civilization had not advanced to the stage of using currency and coins.

A most controversial issue today is the origins of the *varna* system, which divides society into higher and lower castes. In many places in the verses, this term is associated with the Dasas and Dasyus. Many European scholars advanced the idea that the Dasa and Dasyus mentioned in the Rig Veda were actually dark-skinned native people who were displaced by the fair-skinned Aryans. However, it appears that there were differences even within the Aryan tribes in terms of languages, religious practices and other aspects. There is mention of Brahmin and Kshatriya. But they are not associated with the term *varna*. There is no indication yet of castes based on birth and an endogamous system of marriage. The earliest reference to a caste-based division can be seen in the *Purusha Sukta*, which is a later Vedic text and will be covered in the next section.

Nationalist historians and social reformers considered the Vedic age as a golden age for women because of the fact that they worshipped goddesses, there were women sages, women participated in rituals and social life and other such evidence from the Vedic texts. A more thorough analysis of the texts from today's perspective of gender relations has indicated that women were subordinate members of society, patriarchal relations prevailed in the family and women's sexuality and social life were controlled .

Who Created the World?

Many verses in the Rig Veda relate to speculation about the origin of the universe and the creator of all things in the universe. There is a mention of a *brahman* who is self-born and who is manifested in all creatures and who exercises supremacy over all of them. There is also a conception of a supreme man (*Purusha*) in the Rig Veda who pervades all living beings in the world.

Rig Vedic gods had not yet attained individual personalities. They represented the diverse forces of nature. Since forces of nature like rain, thunder and storms have a close relationship with one another, so do the gods who represent them. Many verses in the Rig Veda use the same epithets for the gods. The descriptions of the gods are the descriptions of the forces of nature themselves.

For example, a verse describes the god of fire, or Agni:

> *All-searching is his beam, the gleaming of his light,*
> *His, the all-beautiful, of beauteous face and glance,*
> *The changing shimmer like that floats upon the stream,*
> *So Agni's rays gleam over bright and never cease.*
>
> *(Rig Veda, I.143.3)*[1]

Towards the later period of the Rig Veda, the conception of a supreme lord (Prajapati) started taking shape. The supreme being was called the golden egg (Hiranyagarbha). A verse in the Rig Veda starts to speculate on the origin of the universe:

Then there was neither being nor not-being.
The atmosphere was not, nor sky above it.
What covered all? And where? By what protected?
Was there the fathomless abyss of waters?

Then neither death nor deathless existed;
Of day and night there was yet no distinction;
Alone that one breathed calmly, self-supported,
Other than It was none, nor aught above It.

(Rig Veda X.129)[2]

We find that even as far back as 3000 years, there was a philosophical yearning to understand the creation of the universe, the state of being and non-being that prevailed before this and the series of actions unleashed at the time of creation, including the primeval egg from which the universe is supposed to have evolved.

There are initial thoughts in the Rig Veda that the soul could continue to exist after the body dies. But the idea of the soul transmigrating to another body is not clearly developed. There are suggestions that if sacrifices are performed well, the soul receives a reward, and if not, punishment. One can find the rudiments of the moral idea of a person being rewarded or punished according to his or her good and bad deeds since the state had not fully developed the notion of an inviolable law and order was still in its infancy. Later on, the law of karma and the doctrine of transmigration would become the basis of law and order. The idea of the *atman* was being developed. First, it meant the 'vital breath' in living beings. It would further develop into the self of the world and then the self in man. This is the embryo from which later thoughts that the self of man constitutes the omnipresent supreme principle of the universe would emerge. The knowledge of this self then became the gateway to liberation, *moksha*.

While broadly accepting that the universe was the creation of a supreme being, there was no dearth of agnostic thoughts in the Rig Veda such as 'Who knows whether the world was ever created or not?'

Key Takeaways

- The period 1500–600 BCE encompasses the early and later Vedic periods, reflecting a transition from urbanism to a pastoral society in the Indian subcontinent.
- The Vedas, consisting of Samhitas like the Rig Veda, underscore the tribal and pastoral origins of the Vedic civilization.
- Vedic society was tribal and pastoral, characterized by clans and conflicts, with governance structured around a chieftain and tribal assemblies.
- Economic activities in Vedic society were predominantly pastoral, supplemented by agriculture and plunder, with communal property-sharing practices.
- Manufacturing activities, barter and societal organization around tribal chieftains and assemblies were prevalent in Vedic society.
- The origin of the *varna* system and gender relations in the Vedic society remain debated topics with references to caste-like divisions evolving over time.
- The Rig Veda speculates on the creation of the universe, emphasizing the supreme being (*brahman*) and forces of nature deified as gods like Agni, Surya and Indra.
- Early Vedic thoughts on rewards, punishment, moral deeds and the concept of the self (*atman*) as a pathway to liberation (*moksha*) are evident.
- The Rig Veda reflects agnostic musings on the creation of the world, contemplating uncertainties about its origins.

Fact Check (Answers at the back)

1. What characterized the transition in Vedic civilization from the early to the later period? A) A shift from pastoral to urban settlements B) Evolution from the Iron Age to the Bronze Age C) Transformation from an agricultural to trading economy D) Change from tribal to monarchical governance
2. Which Vedic text contains verses primarily related to spells and incantations? A) Rig Veda B) Sama Veda C) Yajur Veda D) Atharva Veda
3. Which Vedic deity is described in the Rig Veda as representing the forces of fire? A) Agni B) Surya C) Indra D) Varuna
4. How was leadership in Vedic society structured? A) Monarchical rule B) Elected tribal chieftains C) Hereditary kingship D) Oligarchic councils
5. What economic activities were prevalent in Vedic society? A) Trading and currency use B) Agriculture and pastoralism C) Artisan crafts and industry D) Plantation agriculture and serfdom
6. What is a significant feature of the Vedic understanding of rewards and punishment? A) Belief in karma B) Enforced by legal codes C) Based on community consensus D) Decided by the ruling elite
7. Which concept reflects Vedic philosophical thoughts on the creation of the universe and the self? A) Atman B) Paramatman C) Brahman D) Nirguna
8. What was a common sentiment expressed in the Rig Veda regarding the creation of the world? A) Certainty of divine authorship B) Agnostic scepticism C) Mythical allegory D) Scientific explanation
9. Which Vedic deity was associated with the golden egg (Hiranyagarbha) in later Vedic texts? A) Varuna B) Agni C) Prajapati D) Indra

4

The Early Upanishads: Path to Knowledge and Salvation

The four Vedas constitute the Samhitas, sacred commandments handed over from above. The Samhitas were followed by the Brahmanas, the Aranyakas and the Upanishads.

Timeline of

Post-Vedic Literature

900–700 BCE	Brahmanas
Sama Veda	1200–800 BCE
1000–1400 CE	Upanishads
Brihadaranyaka Upanishad	700–600 BCE
700–600 BCE	Chandogya Upanishad
Kena Upanishad	c. 500 BCE
c. 500 BCE	Isha Upanishad

The Brahmanas are documents in prose that explain the importance of various rituals. At the time of the compilation of the hymns of the Vedas, rituals and sacrifices may not have had as much importance as in the later Upanishad period. In a way, the Brahmanas were useful for householders to conduct rituals.

The Aranyakas are forest treatises meant for older citizens who had retired to the forests and who could not perform elaborate rituals. The lesser emphasis on rituals gave way to more philosophical speculations. This led to the compilation of the Upanishads starting from about 1000 BCE. The earliest Upanishads, the Brihadaranyaka and Chandogya Upanishads are believed to have been composed in the seventh to sixth century BCE before the Buddha.

The Upanishads were completely different. They speculated about the path to knowledge and salvation rather than getting involved in the day-to-day activities of priests and followers. Vedic teachings imposed commandments and duties on the people. The Upanishads, however, did not demand any action. Instead, they were concerned about discovering the ultimate truth and the knowledge of reality. So, in the Upanishads, one would find almost an aversion to sacrificial duties. Shankara, the most prominent exponent of the Upanishads, believed that they were meant for people who had already crossed the lower stage of rituals and entered the higher stage of seeking knowledge.

Shruti, Smriti and Sutras

Shruti and Smriti are two types of Vedic literature.

Shruti, which means 'to hear', is canonical and eternal and includes the Vedas, Brahmanas, Aranyakas, and Upanishads. Shruti literature is a product of divine revelation.

Smriti texts are based on human memory and tradition. The Ramayana, Mahabharata and the Pruranas are examples.

Sutras are ancient Indian texts that contain teachings, principles, and guidelines on various subjects such as philosophy, spirituality, ethics, and meditation. They are written in a concise and aphoristic style, making them easy to remember and recite. Some examples are the Yoga Sutras and Brahma Sutras.

To understand the philosophy of this period, we must become familiar with the changes taking place in the economic sphere.

Between 1000 and 600 BCE, the pastoral economy had changed into an increasingly agricultural one. The clans owned larger tracts of land and generated larger surpluses of agricultural produce. The small tribal assemblies had given way to the formation of republics and kingdoms. Many political units coalesced to form kingdoms. The Purus and Bharatas formed the Kuru kingdom. Likewise, the Turvashas and Krivis fashioned the Panchala kingdom. Surplus from agriculture fuelled the second phase of urbanization in the Gangetic belt, the first phase having occurred many centuries back during the mature phase of the Indus Valley Civilization. Rudiments of taxation appeared. Though a fully formed state had not yet come into being, increasing wealth disparity among the population necessitated coercive measures. The *rajan* (king) and the *purohit* (priest) formed a close relationship, justifying each other's existence. The *purohit* led the coronation ceremony of the king. Though the divine right of kings to rule was not recognized, kingship was hereditary, and the king was promoted as a representative of god.

It is believed that the Kuru kingdom was the first political state in India. It was their king, Parikshit, who ventured into gathering the Vedic documents into a canon.

Vedic knowledge did not remain the preserve of the educated Brahmins alone. Many episodes in the Upanishads bring out the involvement of Kshatriyas and other castes in philosophical speculation. Though the Brahmanas were the base for the Upanishads, we find that they were not dominated by Brahmanical thought alone. Later, we will find that various other schools of thought, such as Buddhism, Jainism and the Charvakas, rejected Vedic teachings and ventured out on their own. Thus, this was a period of churning in philosophic thought, the rising non-Brahmanical sections challenging the authority of the Vedic scripts, practices and outlook.

> **Some Key Concepts**
>
> The word *brahman* stands for prosperity and vitality. The Upanishads state that it is a difficult concept to comprehend. It is that which creates living beings, sustains them and to which they return after death. It is eternal and imperishable. The *brahman* 'sees but cannot be seen, thinks but cannot be thought of, perceives but cannot be perceived'.
>
> The *brahman* is the ultimate reality pervading the entire universe. Likewise, the *atman* is the ultimate reality which resides in living beings. It is the imperishable self. When the body dies it transmigrates to another. It has similar qualities as the *brahman*.

The Key to Liberation

The Upanishads were the key to liberation. Though difficult to understand, let alone instruct others on it, they represented the sum of all knowledge at that time. Because of its high level of complex concepts, it could be mastered by only a select few, who then become candidates for liberation from the endless cycle of birth and rebirth (*samsara*). To master the Upanishads one has to take part in debates and discussions so that the essence of the texts is revealed to them.

The earlier Upanishads are in prose. The later ones are in verse. The early Upanishads such as the Brihadaranyaka and Chandogya were probably compiled between 1000 and 500 BCE. The texts explain various aspects of the various schools of Indian philosophy and outlook, which prevail even today, such as ideas of the soul, rebirth, karma, *brahman* and *atman*.

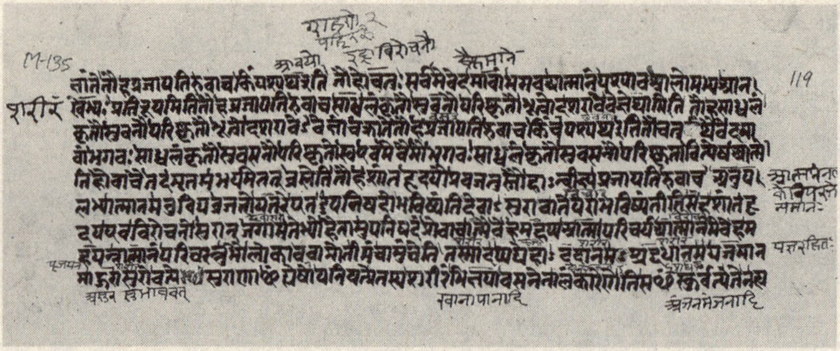

***Figure 2:** Chandogya Upanishad sample, 1865 CE manuscript*

From Vishwakarma to the Atman

We have seen that the verses in the Rig Veda do not all belong to the same period. Some of the books were written much later. In the later verses, the idea of a supreme god takes shape. Prajapati is termed as the lord of beings. Another deity, Vishwakarma, was also promoted as the creator of all beings.

> *Who is our father, our creator, maker,*
> *Who every place doth know and every creature,*
> *By whom alone to gods their names were given*
> *To him all other creatures go to ask him.*
>
> *(Rig Veda, X.82.3)*

During the Upanishad period, a complete transition is made from worshipping forces of nature, such as wind, sun and rain, to a supreme god with absolute powers. The idea of the supreme being as an outside creator of the universe is not pursued. Instead, the attention turns inwards, to the self and the quest for the highest truth. The emphasis turns from the objective to the subjective. In the philosophical discussions that took place, there were many instances of Kshatriyas and women taking an active part.

Atman and Brahman

The Upanishads were written by many authors from different corners of the subcontinent and stretching over many centuries. It is not surprising that they contain widely differing views and ideas.

> **The Meaning of *Atman***
>
> *Atman* means the self or soul within the individual, distinct from the mind, body and senses. It is not possible to perceive it through our senses though we know it exists. Later on, we will come across various interpretations of the individual *atman*, its relationship to the universal *atman*, and how the ultimate reality, the *atman*, got itself confused with the perishable body and the illusory external objects.

The Upanishads were the first succinct expressions of the relationship between man and the external world, including forces beyond his comprehension. Concepts like karma, transmigration of the soul, the cycle of birth, death and rebirth, consciousness, *atman*, *brahman*, and so on.

> **The Meaning of *Brahman***
>
> *Brahman* is interpreted as the vital force that pervades the entire universe. It is the eternal and imperishable reality of the universe. It is that from which all beings are born and sustained and to which they return. It is neither created nor destroyed.

The Upanishads express a pluralism of views. Some Upanishads preach *advaita* (monism) and others *dvaita* (dualism). Based on these various schools of thought belonging to the *advaita*, *dvaita*, *bhedabheda* and *vishishtadvaita*, world view of Indians developed.

The Upanishads also express ethical and philosophical theories such as *ahimsa* (non-violence), *satya* (truthfulness), *daya* (compassion), and so on.

Major points of divergence developed on the interpretation of the individual self, the supreme self, external reality and the supreme reality. Yet, the schools of thought that accept Vedic authority are considered the foundation of Hinduism despite their different world views. Other *darshanas* outside the pale of Vedic authority were loosely termed 'atheistic' even though some of them believed in the existence of a soul and later divisions among the schools introduced the concept of god.

The Secret of the Atman

In Discourse 6.12 of the Chandogya Upanishad, the sage Uddalaka uses a graphic metaphor to explain the nature of the *atman* to his son Shwetaketu. Here is the conversation between them, the initiator being Uddalaka.

'Fetch a fruit of that banyan tree.'

'Here it is, sir.'

'Break it.'

'It is broken, sir.'

'What dost thou see there?'

'These are very small seeds, sir.'

'Break one of these, my dear.'

'It is broken, sir.'

'What dost thou see there?'

'Nothing, sir.'

Then Uddalaka continues: 'My child, the Subtle Essence which thou dost not perceive, it is from that Subtle Essence that this large banyan tree grows up. Have faith. my son.'

Uddalaka continues to give other examples of the Self.

Source: *The Chandogyopanishad with the Commentary of Shankara*. pp. 346–47. English translation by Jha, Ganganadha

Non-Brahmanic Influence

Many episodes in the Upanishads describe how Brahmin sages sought the help of Kshatriyas to unravel a particularly complex concept in philosophy. The Upanishads depart in many instances from the regulations described in Brahmana literature. One more point is that there was a lot of philosophic discourse among the people as narrated by works in Pali. There is evidence of a considerable amount of activity among the Kshatriyas, including several kings. The Buddha himself was a Kshatriya and his *sangha*s teemed with Brahmins and Kshatriyas. Therefore, there is reason to believe that the Upanishads are not the exclusive works of Brahmins alone. The Upanishads also represent non-brahmanic thought. However, it should be kept in mind that it would have been the educated and elite sections of society who would have contributed most to the Upanishadic literature.[1]

The Varna System

While kinship ties were the dominant relations during the Vedic period, as society expanded and the economy diversified, class differentiation arose. The means of production became unevenly distributed among the population. To justify the inequality, society was divided into four hereditary sections, which supposedly had their own characteristics suited to certain occupations and roles.

> The relationship between the Brahmins and Kshatriyas was sometimes antagonistic and at other times complementary. It reflected the conflict between the temporal and the spiritual. That the king should take the counsel of the priest (*purohit*) was reiterated in Vedic texts. The on and off relationship between the vedic gods, Mitra and Varuna, is seen as symbolizing the conflict between the two *varna*s, Mitra representing the sacred power and Varuna representing the secular power.

The first mention of the four *varnas* comes from the 'Purusha Sukta' of the Rig Veda, which says that these sections originated from different parts of the body of a primeval giant named Purusha.

Later texts develop the idea of the *varnas* further. The Brahmins and Kshatriyas are on top of the hierarchy, sometimes the former first and sometimes the latter. Vedic texts reveal periodic conflicts between these two *varnas* for supremacy, the conflict between Mitra and Varuna, for instance.

The top three *varnas* were called the *dvija*, twice-born. The males of these *varnas* go through a thread ceremony called the *upanayana*, which marks their graduation to perform ritual practices. The Shudras were at the bottom of the ladder and were ordained to serve the other three *varnas*. Later, others outside the ambit of the *varna* system, such as tribals and forest dwellers, were co-opted into the *varna* system usually at the bottom rung of the hierarchy.[2]

Key Takeaways

- The four Vedas constitute the Samhitas – sacred commandments handed over from above.
- The Samhitas were followed by the Brahmanas, the Aranyakas and the Upanishads.
- The Kuru kingdom was the first political state in India. It was their king, Parikshit, who ventured into gathering the Vedic documents into a canon.
- Between 1000 and 600 BCE, major changes took place in the economy, small tribal units coalesced into kingdoms, the king and the *purohit* formed an alliance and philosophical speculation flourished.
- During the Upanishad period, a complete transition was made from worshipping forces of nature, such as wind, sun and rain, to a supreme god with absolute powers.

- *Atman* means the self or soul within the individual, distinct from the mind, body and senses.
- The *brahman* is the vital force that pervades the entire universe. It is the eternal and imperishable reality of the universe.
- There is reason to believe that the Upanishads are not the exclusive works of Brahmins alone. The Upanishads also represent non-brahmanic thought.

Fact Check (Answers at the Back)

1. What were the Brahmanas primarily focused on in Vedic literature? A) Philosophical speculation B) Ritual explanations C) Ethical teachings D) Political history
2. How did the Aranyakas differ from the Brahmanas in the Vedic texts? A) Geographical focus B) Ritual complexity C) Philosophical content D) Social customs
3. What distinguished the Upanishads from the Brahmanas and Aranyakas? A) Emphasis on rituals and sacrifices B) Speculation on knowledge and salvation C) Cultural history narratives D) Devotional hymns
4. According to the Upanishads, what was the primary focus of seekers on the path of knowledge? A) Daily rituals and sacrifices B) Ethical conduct in society C) Liberation from the cycle of rebirth D) Symbolic interpretations of Vedic gods
5. How did Shankara, a prominent Upanishadic scholar, view the significance of the Upanishads? A) Intended for the elite Brahmins B) Meant for those seeking knowledge beyond rituals C) Suitable for everyday practical applications D) Targeted at rulers and political leaders
6. What shift occurred in the Indian economy between 1000 and 600 BCE according to the chapter? A) From agriculture to pastoralism B) From pastoral to increasingly agricultural C) From urbanization to nomadic lifestyles D) From barter to coin-based economies
7. Which Vedic document initiated the classification of society into *varnas* in ancient India? A) The Rig Veda B) The Upanishads C) The Aranyakas D) Purusha Sukta

5

Ajivika: Determinism Has Its Sway

Around the sixth century BCE, several changes took place in the Gangetic plains. New kingdoms rose over the ruins of republics. After the first urbanization of the Indus Valley period, a second phase of urbanization gave rise to cities and towns, attracting artisans and craftsmen from villages and destroying their kinship. A powerful lobby of traders and merchants emerged, which challenged the domination of Brahmins and the existing *varna* hierarchy. The newly rising social and economic groups aspired for a philosophy that was in tune with their aspirations. In response to this, several schools of thought arose, which opposed existing religious beliefs and practices and opened up space for new philosophical speculation.

Among the schools that became influential in this period was the Ajivika school. The founder of the Ajivika school of philosophy was Makkhali Gosala (died 484 BCE). Buddhist and Jain documents are an important source about this school, though their accounts may not be entirely reliable.

Figure 3: *An Ājīvika ascetic in a Gandhara sculpture of the Mahaparinirvana, circa 2nd–3rd century CE*

The fact that Ajivikas are mentioned in Buddhist and Jain books shows that the sect must be at least as old as its more established counterparts.

The origins of the sect are still a mystery, but it is generally accepted that the sect was founded around the fifth century BCE.

Buddhist and Jain texts do not speak well of Gosala, probably due to the intense competition that prevailed among the sects that preached asceticism. Jain texts such as the *Bhagavati Sutra* describe Gosala as someone of low birth, an offspring of poor parents and who was born in a cowshed (hence the name Gosala) since the parents had no other place to go. The estrangement that the Jain texts reveal may have its source in the fact that Gosala was at one time a disciple of Mahavira, who accompanied him in his travels for many years and then parted ways with him. The texts often play him down as someone inferior to Mahavira in erudition. The Buddhist texts are no less unkind. Buddhaghosha, the fifth-century commentator, reiterates that Gosala was born in a cowshed and further adds that he was a slave, too.

Are the Ajivikas Fatalists?

In terms of philosophical outlook, the Ajivikas were determinists.

> **Alexander meets the gymnosophists**
>
> When Alexander the Great marched into India, his army met a group of naked wandering saints. The Greeks called them gymnosophists, i.e., wandering philosophers.
>
> Alexander himself is reported to have met some of the gymnosophists himself. Other philosophers such as Pyrrho, who founded the philosophical school of Sceptics were also intrigued by the naked fakirs.
>
> Since the Jains and Ajivikas preached nudity, it can be surmised that the naked philosophers who met Alexander were from these sects. In a way, nudity represented a liberation from all material attachments in Indian thought.
>
> The interest that the Greeks showed was not accidental since they themselves were not new to the practice of nudity. Among them, the Spartans practised nudity. The Olympic Games allowed only naked male participants. The Greek gymnasiums, where naked people exercised, were also a gathering place for philosophers.

They believed that *niyati* (fate) controlled everything and that human effort was pointless. They believed in the Vedic concept of karma and transmigration but insisted that human effort cannot change karma or stop rebirth. To them, the future paths of all souls had already been worked out. What we know of the Ajivika philosophy is from Jain and Buddhist works. The fact that the Ajivika sect was very popular and that the Buddhists and Jains considered the Ajivikas as a serious rival raises the question of whether the portrayal of the Ajivikas as pessimistic and fatalistic is valid. It is very likely that the Ajivikas were not very different in philosophical outlook from their Sramanic counterparts such as Buddhists and Jains.

The Break-Up between Mahavira and Gosala

Jain texts describe incidents that portray Gosala in a poor light.

One such incident occurred when Gosala and Mahavira were walking together. When they came across a plant, Gosala asked Mahavira about the fate of the plant. Mahavira predictably replied that the plant would grow to give fruit, which, in turn, would give seeds for new plants.

Gosala wanted to prove to his master that the plant's fate could be changed. He paid a stealthy visit in the night and uprooted the plant. But a sudden shower caused the plant to sprout again. The incident impacted Gosala so much that it might have given him the idea that everything is ordained, that even the dead can be revived if that is what fate determines.

Mahavira dismissed this theory and that seems to have led to their parting company.

Though the works of the Ajivikas are now lost, we get glimpses of their philosophy from Buddhist and Jain texts. However, these descriptions cannot be taken as unbiased and authentic because of the adversarial relations prevailing among these sects.

The Ajivikas seemed to be a well-organized sect, having regular meetings called *sabhas*, not unlike other sects of the same period. While they practised severe asceticism, often to the envy of other sects, their practice of ahimsa (non-violence) was not as strict as the Jains according to whom meat eating was allowed in the Ajivika sect.

The Ajivikas, like their Buddhist and Jain counterparts, opposed caste hierarchy. Hence, one can find ascetics and the laity from all castes in the Ajivika sect. There were wagon makers, potters and other artisans and craftsmen in their ranks. The sect attracted traders, who were an emerging force and who had to fight against the rigid Vedic orthodoxy to assert themselves. The sect won the allegiance of many powerful kings, such as Prasenajit, the king of Kosala.

The Ajivika sect, like that of the other Sramanic[1] sects, lasted for many centuries and spread to new areas, including as far south as Sri Lanka.

During the period of the Mauryas, the Ajivikas received a lot of support. Ashoka built many caves for the ascetics of the sect, including the Barabar Caves. The edict in his seventh pillar advises officers of the regime to provide support to the Ajivikas along with other Sramanic sects. Arthashastra, a text composed during the Mauryan period, mentions the Ajivikas as an important sect.

In south India, the sect survived very long till the fourteenth century, as evidenced in inscriptions. The Ajivikas are mentioned in the Tamil Sangam Age epics such as Silapathikaram. The parents of Kannagi, the heroine of the epic, are associated with the sect. Kannagi, who later gave rise to the Pattini goddess culture in the Tamil region, had followers from the Ajivika sect.

Ashoka Builds Caves for the Ajivikas

The Barabar Hill Caves are the oldest surviving rock-cut caves in India, dating from the Mauryan Empire (322–185 BCE).

Emperor Ashoka (304–232 BCE) built the caves of Sudama and Vishwakarma in the Barabar Hill, in present-day Jehanabad District of Bihar, for the use of ascetics belonging to the Ajivika school of philosophy. Inscriptions confirm this.

It is believed that Ashoka supported the Ajivikas before he became a full-fledged adherent of Buddhism.

The caves consist of two chambers, carved entirely out of granite and sporting a highly polished internal surface.

Figure 4: *Ancient Barabar Cave Hills – the world's oldest surviving caves*

Purana Kassappa

The Buddhist 'Saamannaphala Sutta' talks about various philosophers who were contemporaries of the Buddha and his rivals in philosophic discourse. It describes an incident when King Ajatashatru wanted some advice from learned saints. His courtiers mention several names such as Makkhali Gosala,

Purana Kassappa and Ajita Kesakambali. These ascetics were contemporaries of the Buddha and Mahavira and were known for their non-conformist views. Finally, Ajatashatru chose to visit the Buddha.

> **Purana Kassappa**
>
> In his commentary on the *Digha Nikaya*, Buddhagosha describes the antecedents of Purana Kassappa.
>
> Kassappa was the hundredth servant in a family of ninety-nine servants. Since he made up the hundredth number, he was called *purana* (completed). For whatever reason, he left the family. On the way, he was unfortunately attacked by thieves, who stole his clothes. Covered only with grass, he ventured into a village. The villagers mistook him for an ascetic. He then actually became a wise man with many followers.
>
> Modern scholars have questioned this description and have pointed out that Kassappa is a Brahmin *gotra*, and hence, Purana must have come from a Brahmin family. But others assert that this *gotra* was prevalent even outside the Brahmin circle.
>
> In another Buddhist text, it is claimed that Purana committed suicide. Considering that Purana's views bordered on nihilism and he must have led a life of futility and frustration, his suicide cannot be ruled out.

King Ajatashatru had murdered his father, King Bimbisara, and captured the throne. His mind was disturbed, and he was in search of peace. When he reached the grove in which the Buddha was sitting with his monks around him, he exclaimed, 'May my son, Prince Udayibhadda, enjoy the same peace that is prevailing now in this community of monks!'

The king described a number of craftsmen who worked hard and were able to enjoy the fruits of labour in this world. He wanted to know from the Buddha whether ascetics could also enjoy the fruits of their contemplative life in this world. Basically, he wanted to know whether asceticism was worth it.

The Buddha wanted to know whether the king had put this same question to any other ascetic. The king admitted that he had approached Purana Kassappa, who was popularly known as a wise man, and put the same question to him. The Buddha was eager to know what the response was.

The king replied that Kassappa answered him this way:

'To him who acts, O king, or causes another to act, to him who mutilates or causes another to mutilate, to him who punishes or causes another to punish, to him who causes grief or torment, to him who trembles or causes others to tremble, to him who kills a living creature, who takes what is not given, who breaks into houses, who commits dacoity or robbery or highway robbery or adultery or who speaks lies, to him thus acting, there is no guilt. If with a discus with an edge sharp as a razor, he should make all the living creatures on the Earth one heap, one mass, of flesh, there would be no guilt thence resulting, no increase of guilt would ensue. Were he to go along the south bank of the Ganges, striking and slaying, mutilating and having men mutilated, oppressing and having men oppressed, there would be no guilt thence resulting, no increase of guilt would ensue. Were he to go along the north bank of the Ganges giving alms and ordering gifts to be given, offering sacrifices or causing them to be offered, there would be no merit thence resulting, no increase of merit. In generosity, in self-mastery, in control of the senses, in speaking truth there is neither merit, nor increase of merit.'

The king then went on to tell the Buddha that he was not happy with the explanation.

It is quite possible to derive from the above conversation that Kassappa advised the king to perform his duties as a king and not become a mendicant who controls his senses and lives an ascetic life.

Makkhali Gosala

King Ajatashatru went on to relate his conversation with Makkhali Gosala on the same topic as described above.

Makkhali said:

> 'There is, O king, no cause, either ultimate or remote, for the depravity of beings; they become depraved without reason and without cause. There is no cause, either proximate or remote, for the rectitude of beings; they become pure without reason and without cause. The attainment of any given condition, of any character, does not depend either on one's own acts, or on the acts of another, or on human effort. There is no such thing as power or energy, or human strength or human vigour. All animals, all creatures (with one, two, or more senses), all beings (produced from eggs or in a womb) and all souls (in plants) are without force and power and energy of their own. They are bent this way and that by their fate, by the necessary conditions of the class to which they belong, by their individual nature; and it is according to their position in one or other of the six classes that they experience ease or pain.'

This may be a distorted view of Gosala's, but it is evident that Gosala believed in transmigration, except that he said one's karma can have no effect on the afterlife.

In a later chapter on Lokayata[1], we will come across other philosophers who had similar views. They all seem to suffer from a deep sense of frustration with the prevailing state of affairs. However, Buddhist and Jain texts have not been accurate in describing the individual views of these philosophers. Different shades of opinion have been attributed to the same philosopher. And the same opinion has been attributed to different philosophers[2].

In the turbulent times in which Gosala lived, he wanted to understand the world he lived in. Huge transformations were happening in the economy, and tribal republics were withering away, giving rise to kingdoms and empires. The state had overwhelming powers. Kings and other elite members of society were living a life of luxury. Urbanization caused the gap between the rich and poor to widen further. The Buddha and Mahavira realized that not much could be done about the inevitable fallout of economic changes. So, they propagated that the way to overcome misery is to realize that nothing is permanent and liberate oneself from material attachments. Philosophers like Gosala faced the new reality and explained that no human action can stop the colossal forces of *niyati* (fate)[3].

Historic Transformations in the Sixth Century BCE

In the sixth century BCE, there were big changes happening in the area that is now Uttar Pradesh and south Bihar. Two big kingdoms, Kosala and Magadha, were getting bigger. They had recently taken over smaller states like Kasi and Anga.

North of these kingdoms were smaller groups of people trying to keep control of their land against the big kingdoms. One of these smaller groups was the Sakyas, who were under the control of the king of Kosala. Another group, the Vajjis, was a group of smaller republics. But soon, these smaller groups were taken over by the big kingdoms.

At that time, people in the region called themselves Aryans. The Buddha, who lived during this time, used the word 'Aryan' to mean 'good' or 'noble'. But even though they called themselves Aryans, there were still a lot of people and ideas from different cultures.

Some people think that the changes happening in religion and philosophy during this time were because non-Aryan people were reacting against the Aryan way of life. The Aryan way of life had strict rules about society and religion.

In this time, some people believed that everything that happened to them was already decided and they couldn't change it. The Ajivika sect, for example, believed that human effort didn't make any difference. This idea might have been popular because life was hard, and people felt like they had no control over things like floods, droughts, and famines, which happened often.

Key Takeaways

- The founder of the Ajivika school of philosophy was Makkhali Gosala (died 484 BCE). He is believed to be a contemporary of Mahavira. Purana Kassappa was another well-known teacher.
- Original Ajivika documents are lost. Buddhist and Jaina documents are an important source about this school, though their accounts may not be entirely reliable. They do not speak well of Gosala, probably due to the intense competition that prevailed among the sects that preached asceticism.
- It is generally accepted that the sect was founded around the fifth century BCE.
- In terms of philosophical outlook, the Ajivikas were determinists. They believed that *niyati* (fate) controlled everything and that human effort was pointless.
- However, the fact that Buddhism and Jainism considered the Ajivikas as a threat implies that their philosophy may not have been very different from the Sramanic schools.

- They were an organized sect that believed in asceticism and opposed caste hierarchy. They received support from the Mauryan kings. They spread to many areas, including south India and Lanka.
- The source of the determinist views of the Ajivikas may be the nature of the turbulent times the school was founded, characterized by the rise of empires and cities and the destruction of tribal republics.

Fact Check (Answers at the Back)

1. The founder of the Ajivika school of philosophy was Makkhali Gosala. (Yes, No)
2. Documents belonging to the Ajivika school exist. (Yes, No)
3. Buddhist and Jaina descriptions of the Ajivika school are authentic (Yes, No)
4. The Ajivika sect was disorganized and had a poor following. (Yes, No)
5. Emperor Ashoka supported the sect and built caves for their ascetics. (Yes, No)
6. Gosala and Kassappa are believed to be contemporaries of the Buddha and Mahavira. (Yes, No)
7. Ajivikas are mentioned in the Tamil epics of the Sangam Age. (Yes, No)
8. The Ajivika philosophy can be characterized as:
    a. Deterministic
    b. Agnostic
    c. Vedic
    d. Spiritual
9. Ajivika philosophy was a reaction to the turbulent times witnessed in the second half of the first millennium BCE. (Yes, No)

6

Buddha: The Causal Chain

Buddhism and Jainism, though popularly classified as religions today, were more of a way of life in their early stages. They advocated the moral and spiritual values and the philosophic outlook of their times. At the same time, their search for a path to salvation – freedom from the perennial cycle of rebirth – takes their teachings beyond the realm of philosophy.

Timeline of Buddhism

563–483 CE	Gautam Buddha, founder of Buddhism
80 CE	Ashvagosha: Early proponent of Vijnanavada
2nd Century CE	Madhyamaka school founded by Nagarjuna
4th to 5th Century CE	Yogachara school: Traditionally ascribed to two half-brothers, Asanga and Vasubandhu

The Buddha (563–483 BCE) concentrated on ethical teaching rather than on metaphysical speculation. For him, the cause of sufferings in this world and the way to attain salvation from these sufferings were more important than such questions as to whether the soul existed even after the body died, whether it could transmigrate to another body, whether the world was finite or infinite, and other such questions. The wish to understand nature that the Vedic people exhibited was not the central focus of Buddhist philosophy.

He reiterated that it is a waste of time to discuss problems for which we cannot find sufficient evidence to solve. He detested coming to conclusions with the help of partial evidence or one-sided views, such as the story of the blind men coming to conclusions about the nature of the elephant after touching only one part of the animal. He rejected the metaphysical views of earlier scholars on the grounds that they were subjective, based on partial evidence and uncertain sense experiences.

> **The ten indeterminate questions of the Buddha:**
>
> 1. Is the world eternal?
> 2. Is the world non-eternal?
> 3. Is the world finite?
> 4. Is the world infinite?
> 5. Are the soul and body the same?
> 6. Are the soul and body different?
> 7. Is there rebirth for one who has mastered truth (*thatagata*)?
> 8. Is there no rebirth for one who has mastered truth (*thatagata*)?
> 9. Does he have both rebirth and no rebirth?
> 10. Does he have both death and life after death?

One who indulges in speculation about the origin of the world while people are suffering in today's world is like the idiotic man who, when struck by a poisoned arrow, wants to know the origin of the arrow and the identity of the bowman before agreeing to get treated.

Therefore, the Buddha emphasized the Four Noble Truths, which will lead people away from going after ethically useless and intellectually uncertain questions and bring their attention to questions concerning the origins of sorrow and the path to put an end to them.

The Four Noble Truths are:

1. Life is full of suffering (*dukkha*).
2. All this suffering has a cause (*dukkha-samusaya*).

3. It is possible to eliminate suffering (*dukkha-nirodha*).
4. There is a path that leads to emancipation from suffering (*dukkha-nirodha-marga*).

The emphasis that the Buddha placed on suffering and the path to freedom from suffering can be understood in the context of the changing social landscape during his time. Large kingdoms were coming into being at the cost of republics. Urbanization and wars uprooted many people from their kinship ties and routine social life in the villages. The status of women deteriorated. Poverty, death and destruction reigned.

The Chain of Twelve Causes

The Buddha analysed the cause of suffering. According to him, misery existed because of some existing conditions, for nothing can exist without the condition for their existence not present. The condition for suffering is birth. If there was no birth, then there would be no suffering, too. But what is the condition for birth? It is the will to be born (*bhava*). What gives rise to this will to be born? It is our attachment to the objects of the world that gives rise to the will to be born. This grasping (*upadana*) of the material objects is the source of the desire to be born. Our thirst for enjoying these objects through our senses, sight, hearing and taste is what stokes this desire. This attachment to the senses arises from our earlier sensory experiences, which make us even more addicted to our sense organs. But sensory experience has a material base. If the sensory organs had not come into contact with objects, then there would have been no sensory experiences. The six organs we use for cognition are a part of the mind–body organism without which sensory organs cannot function. Man acquires this sensory consciousness in the mother's womb, but this consciousness is based on the impressions of one's past life, which is actually ignorant (*avidya*) about the truth because it has craved rebirth. So, the Buddha concludes that it is ignorance that is the root cause of all suffering.

There is No Effect without a Cause

This conclusion has some repercussions. First, it dismisses the theory that something eternal can exist unconditionally since every effect needs a cause and all existence is linked to a causal chain. Second, it also dismisses the theory that something existing can disappear of its own volition. According to the Buddhist school, all the things we perceive have an existence (they are not an illusion) but are dependent on something else and do not vanish without creating an effect. This is the theory of dhamma, the cosmic law and order.

The causal chain for suffering has twelve links as shown below:

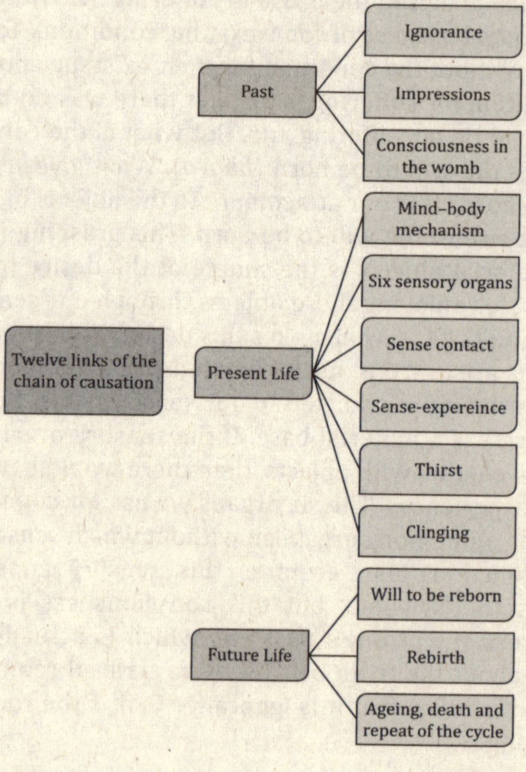

Once the Four Noble Truths are realized, the Buddha defines a path that can be followed both by monks and lay followers, which consists of eight interconnected activities related to knowledge, conduct and concentration or meditation.

The Eightfold Path (Ashtangika Marga), which is a corollary of the fourth Noble Truth, consists of:

1. Right views
2. Right resolve
3. Right speech
4. Right conduct
5. Right livelihood
6. Right effort
7. Right mindfulness
8. Right concentration

Every effect in this world is dependent on a cause, and therefore, has a conditional existence.

Theory of Impermanence

One of the most important teachings of the Buddha related to the concept of impermanence. According to him, all things and phenomena in the world are changing and transitory. There is nothing permanent in the universe. All beings have to go through the process of birth, old age, sickness and death. When it comes to individuals, the 'I' or 'me' is not permanent. It is actually a series of ever-changing combinations of existence. An individual's life can be compared to a river. Outwardly, it appears that the river is unchanging. But the water drops that constitute the river are always in motion. Therefore, the idea of an unchanging 'I' or 'me' is a misconception.

This conclusion logically leads to another conclusion – that there are no eternal substances in the world such as the *atman*, the soul or the universal unchanging self, which, after the death of an individual, transmigrates to another body.

> **Ashoka: The Greatest Patron of Buddhism**
>
> Both the Buddhist texts and Ashoka's inscriptions vouch for the support that Emperor Ashoka gave to Buddhism. He generously contributed to the establishment of *sanghas*. It is said that he ordered 84,000 stupas and *viharas* to be built in all the regions of his empire. He created a sacred map of the places where the Buddha visited and preached. He also made vigorous efforts to spread the message of Buddhism far and wide. His inscriptions talk about the Buddhist dhamma – the rules of conduct. It is said that he sometimes intervened in *sangha* affairs to prevent factionalism and bring harmony to their functioning.
>
> Ashoka himself confers in his inscriptions that he became a pacifist after being influenced by Buddhist teachings. Buddhist texts also describe that Ashoka was a vile ruler until he came under the influence of Buddhism. This coming under the influence of Buddhism cannot be treated as 'conversion' in the modern sense of the term. In the early days, there were no mutually exclusive religious identities and isms.
>
> Buddhist chronicles talk about the third Buddhist Council that Ashoka convened in Pataliputra. The first council was held at Rajagriha, near Patna, after the Buddha's death. The second one was convened at Vaishali after a hundred years. However, Ashoka's inscriptions are silent on the third council.

Karma and Nirvana

Both the Upanishads and Buddhist philosophy believe in the doctrine of rebirth. It is because of karma that there is a difference between human beings. Some live longer than others, some are rich and others are poor, some are powerful, others weak, some wise and some foolish.

The theory of karma (*kamma* in Buddhism) follows directly from the theory of Dependent Origination that we saw earlier. The conditions of the present existence of an individual are the effect of the karma of his or her past lives. Similarly, their future existence will be determined by their karma in this life. This cycle is the reason for all the suffering in this world.

But not all karma produces an effect. If karma is performed without avarice and greed, then the effects become non-existent and the deeds are incapable of bearing good or bad fruits. Preoccupation with the cravings and pleasures of life is the reason for sorrow. When the craving ceases, then the deeds also bear no good or bad fruit. This is what an *arhat* (one who has reached the highest stage of liberation) experiences.

Karmas can be reaped through the body, speech and mind. Mental karma is the root of all the other karmas.

The destruction of all desires leads to nirvana (*nibbana* in Buddhism). However, the Buddhist school avoids discussing the real meaning of nirvana. Nirvana is the state where all sorrow has been extinguished and worldly experiences have ceased to have any meaning. As we will see in the story of Khema in a later section, discussing whether, after nirvana, an individual exists or does not exist in any form is heretical.

Give up the False View about the Self

Some schools of thought believe in the existence of a soul (*atman*) that is eternal, exists before a body's birth and death and migrates from one body to another like the insect that has reached the end of a leaf and deftly moves on to the next. Since the Buddha believed in conditional existence and universal change, he dismissed the idea of an eternal soul, which supposedly is neither the cause nor the effect.

Nagasena and the Chariot

King Milinda (Meander) was a Bactrian king (125–95 BCE) and a well-known dialectician but was not very impressed with Buddhist philosophers until he met Nagasena.

When the king asked him his name, the monk announced that it was Nagasena but added immediately that it was only a label and should not be associated with anything eternal like a soul. This was just a name that his parents had given him.

The king was puzzled by his reply. *How can a body exist without an invisible, permanent soul,* he wondered. *If we don't have a soul, then why worry about our passions and the consequences of our actions? How can a person in this birth be rewarded for his actions in a previous birth? Why worry about good and bad karma? Is it not the soul that is a permanent marker for an individual?*

In response, Nagasena questioned the king about his chariot. Was the chariot any particular constituent, like the axle, wheel, frame or yoke? The king answered that none of these by themselves constituted the chariot. Nagasena explained that since no individual part represented the chariot and since the chariot did not exist outside these parts, the chariot was only a general name for the collection of objects that made the chariot. Similarly, Nagasena was only a general name for the collection of *skandhas*. (In Buddhist philosophy, *skandhas* refer to the five compounds that constitute a human being – form, feelings, cognition, volition and consciousness.

The soul is nothing but a general name for awareness generated by the coming together of these five *skandhas*. They are not eternal. Each *skandha* has a conditional existence.

But if the idea of a soul is dismissed, how can the idea of karma, where one's present life is conditioned by his past deeds, be justified? How is the memory of these deeds carried from one life to another? The Buddha explains this by saying that life itself is composed of a stream of successive states, cause and effect following each other in quick motion. This continuity of the stream of successive states applies to a person's past, present and future life. The twelve-step causal chain discussed earlier explains this. It is like a lamp burning throughout the night. At each moment, the flame and the conditions are not the same. To us, it appears as one continuous flame. They are all connected causally to each other.

Therefore, a soul is not required to carry the memories and transmigrate to another body. The death of a body causes the next life in another body. An unbroken stream of consciousness now takes the place of the soul. Memories can be carried forward in this continuous stream of consciousness. The Buddha exhorts his followers not to fall into the trap of believing that there is an eternal soul. No one has seen it or experienced it, and no one has proved its existence. One cannot attain nirvana by making the soul happy. For the Buddha, it is like falling in love with an alluring woman without ever seeing her or confirming her existence. It is like building a staircase to view a palace that never existed. A man is just a collection of various constituents like mind, body and senses. A chariot is a collection of various parts such as axles, wheels and horses. The soul or ego denotes this collection. When the constituents break up, the collection also breaks up.

The Middle Path

After the Buddha's death, it took some time to compile his oral instructions. There were differing interpretations of his doctrines and monastic rules, which were guiding principles for followers of Buddhism. Around 400 BCE or later, the Buddhist school split into many factions, chief among them being the Hinayana (small vehicle) and Mahayana (great vehicle). Hinayana stood closer to the original Buddhist principles and believed that the ultimate goal was the individual's attainment of salvation or nirvana. The Mahayana adherents aimed not just to seek one's own salvation but of all human beings. From the philosophical point of view, the Hinayanists stuck to the Doctrine of Impermanence. But the Mahayanists went further and declared that all worldly things are non-essential, indefinable and void inside. The Mahayanists later split into two lines, the Madhyamaka (or Sunyavada) and the Vijnanavada trends. Both believe that the world is not real and that it consists of fleeting moments. The Vijnanavada adherents also elaborate on the phenomena of consciousness. Ashvagosha (80 CE) was among the greatest teachers of Vijnanavada.

Buddhism spawned about thirty schools that indulged in metaphysical speculation. For want of space, we will be looking at two important schools: the Madhyamaka and the Vijnanavada (or Yogachara) schools.

Figure 5: *A Japanese depiction of Nagarjuna, one of the greatest Buddhist philosophers and the founder of Madhyamaka*

Nagarjuna, who lived in the second century CE, founded the Madhyamaka school. His philosophy is elaborated in the *Madhyamaka Shastra*.

Nagarjuna advocated the famous doctrine of Sunyavada, which is an elaboration of the Mahayana viewpoint that we saw earlier. The popular perception that people have of Sunyavada is that it is a doctrine which argues that nothing is real in the universe, there is only *sunya*, meaning emptiness or vacuity. It is generally confused with nihilism. But on deeper examination of the philosophy we find that Sunyavada does not deny all reality. While it asserts that the phenomenal world we see in front of us is not real, there is a reality beyond it. The only problem is that this higher reality cannot be described in words, it cannot be perceived, and it is beyond the comprehension of ordinary human beings. It is only the phenomenal world that is *sunya*, empty.

But can *sunya* be merely understood as emptiness? Proponents of Sunyavada use the doctrine of Dependent Origination that we saw earlier to describe their standpoint. All phenomenal objects in the universe have a causal relationship and an impermanent, fleeting existence. Since they are dependent on some condition for their existence and they just appear and disappear like the individual frames in a fast-moving video show, they are not real. At the same time, we cannot say that they are therefore unreal. They live somewhere in between, which is indescribable and indeterminable. This state is called *sunyata*. Since this conclusion has been arrived at based on the doctrine of Dependent Origination, Nagarjuna announces that this doctrine is called *sunyata*. In the Buddhist sense, all dhammas (the natural law, all things in the phenomenal world we experience) belong to the state of *sunya*. This theory is also called Madhyamaka, the middle path, because it talks about a state that is neither real nor unreal and has a conditional existence.

Sunyavada can also be regarded as a theory of relativity where the existence of everything in the phenomenal world is conditional upon and relative to other things. Sunyavada points out that no phenomenon that we experience in the universe has an independent existence and character or *svabhava*.

But all this applies only to the phenomenal world, to our daily experiences. Sunyavada says that all these exist between the state of reality and unreality, a state called *sunyata*. When one attains nirvana and grasps this meaning of *sunyata*, what happens? Is nirvana a state of bliss, an unconditional existence, a permanent reality? The Buddha declined to answer this question, saying that this state cannot be understood by those who are outside it, hence our immediate effort should be to understand the unreal nature of this world.

The adherents of Madhyamika dared to tread into this unknown realm. They explain that there does exist a transcendental reality behind this unreal world. In this state, things are free from conditionality and impermanence. Nagarjuna put forward the thesis that there are two truths. The first is experienced by ordinary people who get drawn into attachment towards worldly objects, *samsara*. The second is experienced by only those who have realized *sunyata* and risen to the world of transcendental reality, where there is no change and no conditionality for existence.

These ideas influenced future philosophers of Advaita Vedanta, like Gaudapada, which we will learn about later .

The School of Subjective Idealism

The Yogachara school, which is another offshoot of Buddhist philosophy, agrees with the Madhyamakas that the external world is illusory. But it differs from them in saying that the individual mind (*chitta*) cannot be unreal. If the mind were unreal, then how would the individual be able to arrive at the reasoning of the conditional existence of phenomena in the external world and their unreality? If the mind is unreal, then all reasoning will vanish.

The Yogachara adherents believe that what we see in the external world is only a stream of images in our mind projected outside. The objects in the external world that we experience with our senses actually don't exist.

The Doctrine of Momentariness

Buddhism believes in impermanence; things come into being and then get destroyed in a continuous cause-effect stream. Buddhism also says that all phenomena have a conditional existence and hence cannot be real. The doctrine of momentariness is a corollary of these theories. It states that whatever exists is momentary by virtue of its existence. Though the doctrine must have been developed earlier, the only authoritative text available is authored by Ratnakirthi, who lived in the late tenth century.

This applies to the self also. One may think that since one has existed for a long time, there is a permanent self. But what they do not realize is that the sense of permanence of the soul is our own belief and not a reality. What we call the self is actually made up of a package of thoughts, feelings and beliefs that shows up at a particular moment and then vanishes. The next moment, a similar package appears, but it is not the same as the previous one. These momentary pictures come one after another in fast succession and resemble each other so much that it gives us the feeling of permanency. If we look for a self in this package, we will not be able to find one.

Why do we think that our self has existed for a long time? We can use the analogy of a book on a shelf. I can say that this book has been there for days on my bookshelf. When I say this, I am referring to the book I am perceiving at that moment. But the book I saw yesterday is only a memory. My senses cannot perceive this. So, when I say that this book has been on the shelf permanently, I am confusing the identity of a book I am perceiving and a book in my memory to prove that the book has been on my shelf permanently.

In the same way, any object like a jug or book has a momentary existence. We can perhaps understand this better if we consider the example of a flame from a lighted oil lamp. The flame looks the same to us even though it is changing every moment. In our body, new cells appear and old cells die, our hair falls and new hair grows, yet we think our body is permanent. All objects in the world have a momentary existence, yet the world appears permanent. The same is the case with our self.

Varna and Jati in Buddhism

The Confrontation with Ambattha

The Buddha considered deeds as more important than *varna* and *jati*, but the Kshatriyas were considered superior to Brahmins implicitly.

Once, on his tour, the Buddha arrived at a Brahmin village called Ichchanakala, which had been donated by King Prasenajit to a Brahmin named Pokkharasadi. Wanting to establish superiority over the Buddha, Pokkharasadi sent his best pupil, Ambattha, to check out the Buddha's thirty-two bodily signs of greatness.

Ambattha met the Buddha and asserted that Brahmins are superior to the Sakya clan, which the Buddha belonged to. The Buddha sat him down and narrated the origin of the Sakyas and proved that they were superior to the Kanhayana *gotra* to which Ambattha belonged. The Buddha hastened to add that Kshatriyas were higher in lineage; that it was wisdom and righteousness that determined who was superior. He also cautioned that howsoever great Pokkharasadi may be, he was finally a recipient of a village from the king. The Buddha then delivered a discourse to Pokkharasadi and converted him into his disciple.

Source: Rhys Davids, *Dialogues of the Buddha*, Vol.1: 112-33

Buddhist philosophy was more socially inclusive than the brahmanical one. The Buddha taught that for complete liberation from sorrows, the state of nirvana, it is necessary to give up all social relationships that acted as fetters.

The Buddhist monastery welcomed people from all castes and classes. The *bhikshus* accepted food from all castes. But it could not aim for the abolition of all social pressures because the conditions were not ripe for it.

Buddhism considered *varna*, the caste system, as man-made and not ordained by the scriptures as Vedic orthodoxy preached. The Buddha asserted that all caste distinctions would cease to exist within the monastery. There would be no discrimination in the selection of monks. However, in reality, a large section of the monks came from higher castes and elite families. There was a large membership from the Kshatriya and Brahmin castes, but lesser numbers belonged to lower castes. Buddhists had reverence for Brahmins as wise men.

Buddhism and the Upanishads

The Upanishads assert that the true self (*atman*) is bliss and that it is eternal and indestructible. It neither has a beginning nor an end. Buddhism also believes that if there is a self, it must be bliss because it is eternal. This is quite explicitly stated in Buddhism and somewhat implicitly believed by the Upanishads.

Buddhism also states explicitly that the world of objects is not eternal, and hence, cannot provide bliss. In fact, they are the source of sorrow, and the self needs to be liberated from that.

The Upanishads, on the other hand, argue that the self, which is true and unchangeable, confuses itself with the impermanent world and gets entangled in *samsara*, the cycle of birth and rebirth. This permanent self cannot be described. One can only say that the self is 'not this, not this' (*neti, neti*).

The Story of Khema

Khema, the wife of King Bimbisara (544–492 BCE), emperor of Magadha, was renowned for her beauty. Khema loved anything of beauty, including her own.

Since Bimbisara had great respect for the teachings of the Buddha, he wanted his wife, too, to share his faith. Knowing that she would not easily agree to meet the Buddha, he enticed her by describing the beauty of the garden in the monastery where the Buddha was camping.

Khema was initially annoyed when she knew her husband's real intention, but as the Buddha spoke, she stood rooted to the spot. She saw a woman standing near the Buddha whose beauty made her envious. But to her horror, the woman started ageing until she transformed into a crone. Khema realized with a jolt that this was a message for her. She was so taken in by the Buddha's teachings that she transcended all stages of a nun's life and became an *arhat* (a saint who has reached the highest stage of nirvana) on that very day.

King Pasenadi Kosala, coming to know about the enlightened nun, went to see her. He enquired whether the Buddha did or did not exist after death. Khema replied that the Buddha had not declared whether he would exist or not exist after his death. The king was not amused. Khema explained that just as one cannot count the grains of sand on a riverbed or the volume of water in the ocean, in the same way, the Buddha cannot be fathomed. It is not sure whether 'he exists' or 'he doesn't exist' or 'he both exists and doesn't exist'.The Buddha was exhilarated when he came to know of Khema's response. Khema later contributed poems to the Therigatha, or Verses of the Elder Nuns, a revered work.

Early Buddhism does not see any intermingling of the self with our day-to-day experiences. The world of phenomena is always changing; it therefore leads to sorrow, and that is why it cannot have any connection with the self. The self never confused itself with the non-self, the experiences of the impermanent world were not that of the self, and neither did the self belong to these experiences.

The Upanishads argue that the self is transcendental, beyond human experience, indescribable but exists nevertheless. The Buddha claimed that there was no self, and when someone said they experienced the self, it must be their own mental experiences.

Differences in Indian Philosophical Systems on Cause and Effect

Concerning the relation of cause and effect, the Advaita Vedanta of Shankara propounded that cause alone was permanent and real. All effects are impermanent illusions arising out of ignorance.

The Saankhya doctrine held that there was no difference between cause and effect, except that a cause is the earlier stage of an effect, which, when transformed through certain changes, becomes the cause, and the cycle goes on.

Buddhism argues that everything is momentary. So cause and effect are also momentary. A momentary cause is destroyed to produce a momentary effect. There is no permanent reality.

The Nyaya system does not agree with the Saankhya system. It does not admit that the effect was pre-existent in the cause. The material cause (e.g. clay) possesses some power, and in combination with accessories, such as the wheel, potter and stick, destroys the clay and produces a new effect in the form of a pot. This is the opposite of the Saankhya view that what is existent cannot be destroyed and that what does not exist cannot be produced. Saankhya says that if what is non-existent can be produced, then anything, even a hare's horn, can be produced. Nyaya–Vaisheshika philosophy counters this argument with the explanation that nothing that is non-existent can be produced, but that the effect was not pre-existent in the cause. The pot was not present in the clay. But the clay had some powers which when combined with other inputs such as a potter with a wheel, could be converted into a pot.

These are fundamentally different views on the nature of the world and its objects, the permanence or impermanence of phenomena and whether there was one supreme being that caused the world.

”

The Upanishads believe that the self is immutable, the absolute truth. But for the Buddha, nothing was permanent, and it was impermanence that brought sorrow. Only the realization of the Four Noble truths that we saw earlier can liberate a human being. The Buddha categorically declared that there was no self, no Brahman and ignorance does not belong to an individual self[1].

The Status of Women in Buddhism

Just as we saw the participation of women in the Upanishadic debates, the Buddhist *sangha* also gave space to women to take part in discussions, though a good part of the *bhikkunis*, like the *bhikkus*, may have been from the upper castes. The *sanghas* were open to destitute and orphaned women and those who faced discrimination and oppression in the outside world.

Buddhism acknowledged that women could aspire for nirvana and also form monasteries. At the same time, Buddhist texts did not desist from stereotyping the role of ordinary women as those who should take care of the family and be submissive. The

Buddha himself was reluctant to admit women nuns for fear that they may 'distract' the monks, until his disciple, Ananda, and his foster mother put pressure on him. Celibacy was held in high esteem according to the social mores of the period.

Women had to get permission from their husbands or parents to join a *sangha*. Breastfeeding women were not allowed to join a *sangha*. In the affairs of the *sangha*, nuns had to subordinate to the authority of monks. Nevertheless, there are several references to learned women who were revered in the *sanghas*.

Contact between monks and nuns was regulated, though the monasteries for women were not far away from the men's to ensure their protection. Monks accompanied nuns when they went out to gather alms.

Nevertheless, Buddhism opened up significant space for women. Women played an important role in Buddhist texts. In general, it can be said that considering the conditions around 2500 years back, the Buddhist school adopted a relatively progressive tradition towards women.

Key Takeaways

- Buddhism and Jainism, though popularly classified as religions today, were more of a way of life in their early stages.
- The Buddha concentrated on ethical teaching rather than on metaphysical speculation.
- The Buddha preached that though the world is full of suffering, there is a path to emancipation.
- The Four Noble Truths are the foundational tenets of Buddhism.
- The chain of twelve causes explains the origin of suffering.
- The Eightfold Path serves as a guide to non-attachment and emancipation.

- According to the Buddhist Theory of Impermanence, all things and phenomena in the world are changing and transitory.
- There are no eternal substances in the world such as the *atman*, the soul or the universal unchanging self.
- The Buddha's theory of Dependent Origination says that every effect in this world is dependent on a cause, and therefore, has a conditional existence.
- The conditions of the present existence of an individual are the effect of the karma of his or her past lives. Similarly, their future existence will be determined by their karma (*kamma*) in this life. This cycle is the reason for all the suffering in this world.
- The destruction of all desires leads to nirvana (*nibbana*).
- Around 400 BCE or later, the Buddhist school split into many factions, chief among them being the Hinayana (small vehicle) and Mahayana (great vehicle).
- All phenomena have a conditional existence, and hence, cannot be real. Whatever exists is momentary by virtue of its existence.
- Considering the conditions around 2500 years back, the Buddhist school adopted a relatively progressive tradition towards women.

Fact Check (Answers at the Back)

1. Early Buddhism was related to a lot of metaphysical speculation. (Yes, No)
2. The Buddhist school adopted a relatively progressive tradition towards women. (Yes, No)
3. In Buddhism, nirvana (nibbana) can be achieved by:
    a. Strictly following rituals and sacrifices
    b. Living life to the full
    c. Destruction of all desires
    d. Learning the Vedic texts.
4. Of the following, which is a major Buddhist sect:
    a. Svetambara
    b. Ajivika

c. Mahayana
d. Lokayata

5. According to the Buddhist Theory of Impermanence, all things and phenomena in the world are changing and transitory. (Yes, No)
6. Does Buddhism believe in the cycle of life, death and rebirth? (Yes, No)
7. Buddhism believed in an eternal, unchanging universal self. (Yes, No)
8. Buddhism generally admitted all castes into the *sangha*. (Yes, No)

7

Jain: Reality Is Manifold

The Buddha and Mahavira, the most important of the Jain *tirthankaras*, were contemporaries. So, as one would expect, there are a lot of similarities between their teachings since they were located in the same temporal and cultural space. Both opposed Brahmanical orthodoxy and rejected sacrifices and rituals as the path to attaining salvation. Instead, they preached that there was no god and that it was the efforts of human beings that took them closer to salvation. They preached asceticism, a rejection of the material pleasures of the world. They established a monastic order for male and female ascetics. Ordinary people could be followers without subscribing to the strict rules for ascetics. Both religions did not reject the *varna* system but considered Kshatriyas as having a status above that of Brahmins, even though many monks were from the Brahmin community. But there were also several differences between them, which we will discuss later.

Timeline of

Jain Philosophy

877–777 BCE — Parshvanatha, the twenty-third *tirthankara* of Jainism. He is the earliest Jain *tirthankara* who can be reliable dated.

599–527 BCE — Mahavira, the twenty-fourth and last *tirthankara*.

Jainism is made up of members of the followers of *jina*, one who has conquered knowledge and can lead others to *moksha* – liberation from the endless cycle of birth and rebirth that ordinary mortals are subject to.

Mahavira was not the founder of Jainism. He was, in fact, the last of the twenty-four *tirthankaras*, those who built a ford to help followers cross the vast ocean of suffering. It is said that a tirthankara is born in every half-cycle of the Jain time scale. The first tirthankara was Rishabhanatha. The twenty-third was Parshvanatha. Vardhamana Mahavira was the twenty-fourth. His birth year is estimated to be 599 BCE.

There Is No One Reality

Where the Jains differ from other schools of thought is in their interpretation of reality. Different schools have different views on whether reality is eternal or fleeting, whether it is absolute and unchanging or in flux and whether the objects we see around us are real or illusory. Jainism holds that all these statements represent different views of reality and no one view is entirely true. Reality is manifold, and there is no absolute truth. This, in essence, is the doctrine of *anekantavada*, the manifold instances of reality.

> **The Jain Conception of Substance (*Dravya*)**
>
> According to Jains, there are six eternal substances in the universe:
>
> i) Sentient beings or souls (*jīva*)
>
> ii) Non-sentient substance or matter (*pudgala*)
>
> iii) The principle of motion (*dharma*)
>
> iv) The principle of rest (*adharma*)
>
> v) Space (*akasa*)
>
> vi) Time (*kaala*)
>
> The last five constitute the *ajiva* (non-living).

The doctrine of *anekantavada* argues that any entity is at once enduring but also undergoing change that is both constant and inevitable.

According to *anekantavada*, all entities that exist in the world are composed of three aspects in different proportions – substance (*dravya*), quality (*guna*) and mode (*paraya*).

Another doctrine of the Jainas, *syadvada* (the doctrine of maybe) is a corollary of *anekantavada*. Since reality is manifold, our assessment of an object represents only one possible judgement out of many. So, a judgement cannot be absolute. It has to be always qualified by the circumstances surrounding the judgment. In essence, both doctrines emphasize the fact that reality is a complex phenomenon and it is impossible to grasp it in its entirety.

The Five Great Vows

Once a person is convinced about the Jain faith and its doctrines, they are required to take five vows: i) non-violence (*ahimsa*), ii) truth (*satya*), iii) not to steal (*asteya*), iv) celibacy (*brahmacharya*) and v) non-possessiveness (*aparigraha*).

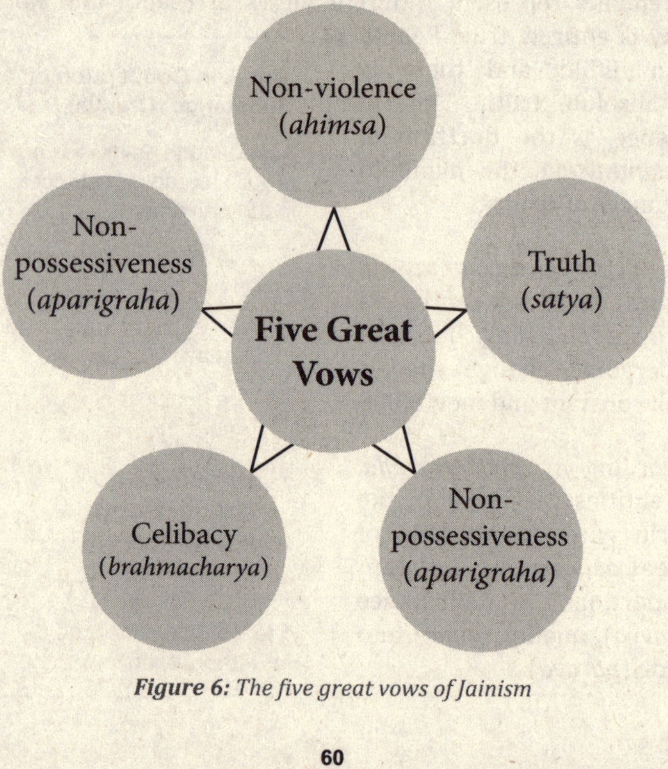

Figure 6: *The five great vows of Jainism*

While all other religions insist more or less on all these moral codes, the tenet of ahimsa is central to Jainism. Injuring living beings, even the tiniest insect, is considered a great sin because it harms innocent victims and also harms the perpetrator of the crime. The Jains go to great extents to honour this tenet. In order to not cause injury to living beings, they are required to be vegetarians and even avoid certain foods like figs, honey and alcohol. Eating animal meat was strictly forbidden, whether the animal was already dead or killed for its meat. But later on, certain concessions were made and meat eating was allowed in times of famine or to cure one's illness. Monks and nuns were required to carry a broom when moving around to brush away insects from being trampled upon.

During the time of Mahavira, he and his disciples moved around naked to emphasize that ascetics cannot have any material attachments and have renounced all their possessions. Later on, after the death of Mahavira, when the Jains split into the Digambara (sky-clad, that is, naked) branch and the Shwetambara (white-clad) branch, the latter discontinued the practice of nudism.

The five vows of good conduct were not applied rigidly to ordinary disciples. While the first three vows applied to them, they were not constrained to practice celibacy. They could lead a married life provided they honoured chastity. For the laity, the last vow of non-posessiveness was watered down to 'limiting one's wants'. So, Jainism, like Buddhism, kept the householders close to them, often relying on them for food, donations and the construction of monasteries.

The strict practice of ahimsa prevented Jains from indulging in many occupations, such as hunting, farming and warfare. Merchants and traders who could afford to practice ahimsa without prejudice to their occupations thrived in the Jain fold. Writing and arts were also preferred occupations.

However, the practice of non-violence was not unqualified. There are instances of Jain monks training themselves and using violence in self-defence or to protect nuns and monasteries.

The Changing and the Unchanging

On the question of changing and unchanging reality, the Jains have differences of opinion with the Upanishadic and Buddhist viewpoints.

If we take the example of clay, it can assume various shapes, such as a pot, brick or sculpture. According to the Chandogya Upanishad, the clay matter that forms the base of all these finished products is the only permanent thing. The various shapes that the clay matter assumes are only different appearances of the original substance, and hence, are mere manifestations of the unchanging original. Therefore, objects that we perceive through our senses are mere illusions, have no real existence and are just different appearances of the unchanging reality.

The Buddhists, on the other hand, hold the opposite view. For them, it is the objects we perceive, the changing qualities of a substance, that are real. All clay objects, including the clay matter out of which they are made, have qualities that can be perceived by the senses. There is no other substance that doesn't possess quality or is unchanging. The existence of an unchanging substance is mere fiction. The qualities of different forms of clay are real, and there is no unchanging substance to which they cling. Therefore, we should regard the world as consisting of different qualities that come and go, which get transformed from one to another.

The Jains, who were contemporaries of both schools of thought, had to join the debate. They advocated a middle path. They did not agree with the Buddhists that there is no permanent substance and that the different qualities of a substance constitute reality. They also did not agree with the opposite view that it is the substance that is permanent and the various qualities it assumes are just sensory illusions. For them, both these views were extreme ones, not in tune with experience. These views were just some elements of truth but not the whole truth itself.

They theorized that some qualities were unchanging, some changed, giving rise to new qualities, and some other qualities disappeared. But while qualities changed there was something unchanging, too. Thus, when a pot is fashioned out of a lump of clay, the lump of clay is destroyed, and a pot is produced with new qualities, but the clay in the pot still retains its qualities. The form has changed, but the underlying quality is still there. Therefore, while things have changed, the quality of clay has been preserved. Similarly, when gold is melted and made into a ring, the form has changed and acquired a new quality at the expense of the old quality, but the quality of the gold has remained unchanged.

The conclusion is that there is something called a permanent entity with permanent qualities even though it changes in form – losing some qualities and gaining new ones.

A One-Sided Viewpoint Is Dangerous (Anekantavada)

The Jain doctrine of *anekantavada* (the viewpoint of many-sidedness) is related to the conception that reality is both changing and unchanging and that it takes several forms that appear and disappear.

The Jains regarded all phenomena as being many-sided. One can have a judgement, but all judgements are true only under certain conditions.

The Buddha believed in the Middle Way. Whenever metaphysical questions were put to him, he rejected extreme viewpoints such as 'it is' or 'it is not'.

For Mahavira, extremes were possible, but he also added the viewpoint 'perhaps'. The Jains believed in the dualistic conception that all living beings were composed of *jiva* (soul) and *ajiva* (matter).

The Parable of the Blind Men and the Elephant

This parable has been quoted in many Buddhist and Jain texts and illustrates the concept of *anekantavada* well.

According to the parable, a group of blind men wanted to know about the elephant. Each blind man groped a different part of the elephant's body and arrived at a different understanding. The one who stroked the trunk exclaimed that it was like a thick snake. The other who touched the ear felt the animal was like a thin fan. The third who felt the elephant's leg concluded that it was built like a tree trunk. The one who got hold of the tail said it was like a rope.

The parable illustrates the point that one's subjective experience cannot account for the entire truth. Truth is relative and applies only to that particular context. It also emphasizes that experts studying a phenomenon need to have a deep understanding and should respect each other's views, for the truth can be arrived at only by putting together all valid viewpoints and experiences.

No phenomenon or object can be affirmed absolutely. A clay jug is a substance (*dravya*) made up of earth atoms. At the same time, it is not a substance like space or time. In that case, it is not *dravya* in another sense. It is not made up of metal atoms or water atoms. It is a breakable *dravya* as compared to an unbreakable one such as a gold pot. Proceeding on these lines,

Jain philosophy believes that judgements are true only in a limited sense in a specific environment[1].

Figure 7: *Jain temple painting explaining Anekantavada with the blind men and an elephant*

Seven Ways to Judge Things (Syadvada)

According to the Jain outlook, the universe, and for that matter any object within it, can have infinite characteristics. So, an imperfect being such as human mortals cannot have knowledge of all those innumerable aspects. Any judgement is based on partial knowledge, like the different views of the seven blind men about an elephant.

Various systems of philosophy have different viewpoints. But they disagree with each other because they think that their viewpoint is the absolute truth, while in reality, there can be infinite viewpoints. The Jains do not think that their viewpoint is the only truth. In fact, they assert that all viewpoints or judgements must be accompanied by a tentative 'perhaps' or 'maybe'.

For example, when someone says that 'there is a pot', it is only a partial truth. The pot may be black or red, short or tall, made of gold or clay. It may be inside or outside the room. So the statement is valid only for a particular instance of the pot in specific conditions of time, space, quantity and quality.

So, Jain philosophy does not simply accept an affirmative or negative answer. They qualify them with seven possibilities:

1. In some ways, the pot is.
2. In some ways, the pot is not.
3. In some ways, the pot is and is not.
4. In some ways, the pot is, and it is indescribable.
5. In some ways, the pot is not, and it is indescribable.
6. In some ways, the pot is and is not, and it is indescribable.
7. In some ways, the pot is indescribable.

The *syadvada* doctrine argues that an object can have contrary characteristics and may appear in infinite varieties, like the pot. Therefore, no affirmation or judgement is absolute in its nature. The Jain concept is often compared with the Western philosophical conceptions of pragmatism and relativity. But they are not the same. The Jain concept is not an idealist outlook; it is based on reality. Neither is it a sceptical doctrine. The Jains do not question the uncertainty of a judgement. All that they say is that the judgement should be qualified as conditional and relative to a specific circumstance.

The Jain outlook may appear as tentative and hazy. But there is no uncertainty about their principles and discipline. The five vows for Jain monks and nuns, for example, are inviolable and there is no 'perhaps' about them.

Is There a God?

Like the Buddha, Mahavira preached that there is no god. Jain philosophy advances the argument that it is our common experience that all products are produced by a creator working his limbs and accessories. If, as the schools like the Nyaya say, god is formless, then how was it possible for him to create the world and its products?

It is said that god is omnipotent and immanent and that he was the cause of all effects in the universe. But we see with our own eyes that products such as a pot and house could be produced without the intervention of god.

Though Jains reject the concept of god, they revere those who have attained liberation, the *siddhas*. Similarly, the *arhats* and Bodhisattva are revered in Buddhism.

The Jiva (Soul)

Jainism believes in the existence of the soul (*jiva*), which has consciousness as its essence. Souls differ according to the degree of consciousness. The soul is eternal, but it also undergoes changes. It is the soul that enables a living being to carry out activities and also experience pleasure, pain and other emotions. It exists independent of the body. Since all parts of the body experience consciousness, the soul, whose attribute is consciousness, also pervades the entire body. The soul can be directly perceived by anyone just as they perceive any external object.

To start with, the soul is in its pure state, a repository of infinite knowledge, bliss and power. But over many cycles of birth and rebirth, the soul gets tarnished by karma matter just as a white cloth gets coated by a layer of dirt. They are infinite in number and fill the body like the light emanating from a lamp fills a room. These souls are differentiated according to the number of sense organs they control. The lowest class is the plant, which has only one sense of touch. The highest are the higher animals, including human beings, who possess all five sense organs, and in addition, the mind (*manas*), which enables them to make rational decisions.

Why are *jivas* born as higher and lower beings? It is due to their accumulated karma, their merits and demerits, that *jivas* are born as men or animals. There are different kinds of karma matter. One type of karma matter prevents the soul from acquiring right knowledge, another from right perception, and so on. Karma determines the biodata of a person, the length of life, body structure, family, caste and other attributes. Our knowledge is not dependent on external objects but limited by our internal karma. After the death of the body, the *jiva*, along with its karmic matter, occupies another body, and the cycle of birth, death and rebirth goes on until the jiva gets rid of the karmic matter and attains *moksha* through right action.

Differences among the Non-Vedic Schools

Even though the three schools of Buddhism, Jainism and Lokayata are considered heretical as they reject the authority of the Vedas, they differ on many aspects, one being the nature of the self or soul (see Table 1).

Social Composition

The Jains, just like Buddhists, considered the Kshatriyas as superior to all other *varnas*. Their texts attribute the creation of the Kshatriya and other *varnas* to the first *tirthankara*, Rishabha. His son, Bharata, created the Brahmin *varna*.

The Jains criticized the rituals, sacrifices and arrogance of the Brahmin priests. But they were not against the *varna*

Comparison of Buddhism, Jainism and Charvaka (Lokayata) schools		
Buddhism	Jainism	Charvaka (Lokayata)
• There is no soul. • There is a continuity of thoughts in different births. But these are not carried by the soul. They are a series of momentary states, like a lamp burning through the night. • Rebirth is not the entry of a soul from one body to another but a causal connection of a stream of consciousness from the past, present and future. • The body is a collection of the material body, the immaterial mind and formless consciousness. When the body dies, this collection breaks up.	• There is a soul. It is present in all parts of the body as consciousness. • It is the soul that drives activities and experiences emotions. • We can perceive the existence of the soul through our immediate experiences just as we perceive a substance through the quality of a substance. • The sense organs cannot function by themselves. There needs to be a driver, and that is the soul.	• Other-worldly entities, such as immaterial souls or gods and the afterlife do not exist. • Consciousness is the product of material elements. • Perception is the only valid source of knowledge. Since we cannot perceive the soul, it doesn't exist. • Not all matter can acquire consciousness. But there is no need for a soul to produce consciousness from matter. • There is no birth and rebirth, there is no transmigration of the soul from one body to another or a stream of consciousness continuing from one birth to another.

Table 1: *Comparison of Buddhism, Jainism and Charvaka*

system itself. Though they opposed Brahmins, the Jain monks themselves aspired to become 'true' Brahmins. According to them, a true Brahmin is not defined by his birth but by his conduct.

The Jain *sangha* welcomed people of all *varnas* and social backgrounds. Even *chandalas* (untouchables) like the monk Harikeshiya found respect in the *sangha*. While Jainism was born out of a reaction against Brahmanical orthodoxy, many of the key disciples of Mahavira were Brahmins who joined en masse from the Magadha region. Many Jaina *acharyas* were Brahmins, such as Bhadrabahu and Haribhadra.

The social base of the Jain order, as in the case of Buddhism, was the affluent urban merchant class who found that Jain philosophy catered to their expectations. These upwardly mobile classes were drawn to emerging philosophies that rejected the superiority of the Brahmins and gave space to other *varnas*.

Similar to the Buddhists, the Jains established a monastic order for women, though Jain texts warn their adherents about the dangers from women to celibacy and warn monks to keep away from them. During the lifetime of Mahavira, it is reported that thousands of women joined as nuns and ordinary followers.

The emphasis on not wearing clothes caused a lot of trouble for women nuns. This continued in the Digambara sect, which had strict rules against wearing clothes. In this sect, nuns were not considered the equals of monks. Women could attain *moksha* only after they were reborn as men. In the Shwetambara sect, which allowed wearing clothes, women were more or less equals and they could attain salvation in their lifetime. They could even become *tirthankaras*. In the Shwetambara tradition, the nineteenth *tirthankara*, Malli, was a woman.

Key Takeaways

- Jainism opposed Brahmanical orthodoxy and rejected sacrifices and rituals as the path to attaining salvation.
- The Jain school did not believe in the existence of a god.
- It preached asceticism, a rejection of the material pleasures of the world.
- Members of the Jain religion are followers of *jina*, one who has conquered knowledge and can lead others to *moksha*.
- The doctrine of *anekantavada* argues that any entity is at once enduring but also undergoing change that is both constant and inevitable.
- According to this doctrine, all substances that exist in the world are composed of three aspects in different proportions – substance (*dravya*), quality (*guna*) and mode (*paraya*).
- The doctrine of *syadvada* asserts that since reality is manifold, our assessment of an object represents only one possible judgement out of many.
- Those who believe in the Jain faith and its doctrines are required to take five vows: i) non-violence (*ahimsa*), ii) truth (*satya*), iii) not to steal (*asteya*), iv) celibacy (*brahmacharya*) and v) non-possessiveness (*aparigraha*).
- Jainism believes in the existence of the soul (*jiva*), which has consciousness as its essence.
- The Jain *sangha* welcomed people of all *varna*s and social backgrounds.

Fact Check (Answers at the Back)

1. The first tirthankara of Jainism is:
    a. Parshvanatha
    b. Mahavira
    c. Rishabhadeva
    d. Makkhali Gosala
2. The doctrine of anekantavada argues that reality is manifold. (Yes, No)
3. One need not take the vow of ahimsa to join the Jain faith. (Yes, No)
4. Mahavira preached that there is no god. (Yes, No)
5. The Jain theory of syadvada believes that a judgement can have seven possibilities. (Yes, No)
6. The Jain *sanghas* allowed only people belonging to higher castes to become members. (Yes, No)
7. According to Jainism, the soul is eternal but also undergoes changes. (Yes, No)

8

Charvaka (Lokayata): This-Worldly and Materialistic

The Charvaka school of philosophy, also called the Lokayata, is considered to rely on materialism as its world outlook. Materialism means that matter is the fundamental substance in nature and all living beings, including mind and consciousness, are created by the interaction of matter. The adherents of this school rejected the existence of souls and the theory of transmigration. They refused to accept any reality other than what was perceived, and that included the existence of a supreme being. They belong to the 'atheistic' group of schools of philosophy including Buddhism, Jainism and the Ajivikas, though they are different from the others in many ways.

Timelines of **the Lokayata school**

Sixth century BCE	Charvaka
Brihaspati	Sixth century BCE
Sixth century BCE	Ajita Kesakambalai

Buddhism, Jainism and the Charvakas started out as schools of philosophy. Buddhism and Jainism evolved over time. Both developed into organized religions with established institutions, scriptures, rituals, and communities of followers. They spread widely and gained significant influence across different regions.

On the other hand, Charvaka philosophy did not develop into an organized religion. It remained primarily as a philosophical school of thought without the institutional structures and widespread community organization that characterize religions. Charvaka philosophy did not leave behind a significant body of scriptures or rituals, which are typical of organized religions.

The ideas of the Charvakas can be traced back even to the later books of the Rig Veda. It is quite possible that this school is even more ancient than Buddhism and Jainism. Just like the Vedic texts, the Charvaka Sutra may have been handed down orally from generation to generation until they were codified around the sixth century BCE.

> **The Meaning of Lokayata**
>
> Lokayata meant the philosophy of the people. It also stood for the philosophy of this-worldliness or materialism.
>
> The Lokayata school took its name from *ayatah* (prevalent) and *lokesu* (among the people).

The Katha and Brihadaranyaka Upanishads talk about people who did not believe that consciousness existed after death. The Chandogya Upanishad refers to a race called the asuras, who believe that the body is itself the soul, and therefore, they adorn dead bodies and provide food so that the dead can dominate the other world.[1] The reference to asuras is often considered as a reference to heretics who did not believe in the Vedic texts.

Madhava, a later Vedanta philosopher, says about the Charvakas:

> In this school, the four elements earth, etc., are the original principles; from these alone, when transformed into the body, intelligence is produced, just as the inebriating power is developed from the mixing of certain ingredients; and when these are destroyed, intelligence at once perishes also.[2]

Madhava links this idea to a verse in the Brihadaranyaka Upanishad:

> Springing forth from these elements, itself solid knowledge, it is destroyed when they are destroyed – after death no intelligence remains.[3]

However, scholars like Dasgupta do not agree that the germs of the ideas of the Charvakas were present in the Upanishads.

Like the Ajivikas, the texts of the Charvakas haven't survived. The primary document of the Charvakas has been mentioned in other sources, such as the Brihaspati Sutra, but this text has not survived. So, one can access the theories of this sect only from secondary sources. The Arthashastra quotes the Brihaspati Sutra. In the epics such as the Mahabharata and the Ramayana, we find discussions centring on the ideas of this school. Buddhist and Jain literature also reveal a certain familiarity with this school. For instance, in the Brihadaranyaka Upanishad, the sage Yajnavalkaya declares that there is no awareness after death, contradicting the Upanishadic position on the transmigration of the soul, the cycle of birth and death, the existence of a supreme being and so on. No wonder that his pupil, Maitreyi, expresses dismay over his statement. All this substantiates the point that the Charvaka school may have predated many other Astika and Nastika schools.

There is controversy over whether Charvaka was the founder of this school or Brihaspati. Another philosopher, Ajita Kesakambali, is quoted in various Buddhist and Jain texts and is believed to have propounded the same theories as the Charvakas. Just as we saw how the Ajivikas and their founder Makkhali Gosala were ridiculed by Buddhists and Jains, Ajita also met with the same fate. There is a legend that he was called Kesakambali, meaning a blanket made of hair, to ridicule him as foul-smelling and uncouth.

Ajita had expressed views on the soul and gifts for the dead body:

> A human being is built up of the four elements. When he dies, the earthly in him returns and relapses to the earth, the fluid to the water, the heat to the fire, the wind to the air, and his faculties pass into space. The four bearers, on the bier as a fifth, take his dead body away; till they reach the burning ground men utter forth eulogies, but there his bones are bleached, and his offerings end in ashes. It is a doctrine of fools, this talk of gifts. It is an empty lie, mere idle talk, when men say there is profit therein. Fools and wise alike, on the dissolution of the body, are cut off, annihilated, and after death they are not.

The World Outlook of the Charvakas

Madhava's interpretation of Charvaka philosophy suggests that they believed only in direct perception as a valid source of knowledge. However, this would make life impossible, as inference plays a crucial role in understanding the world.

Despite this, various texts indicate that Charvakas also valued logic and arguments. For instance, Sukra Niti Sara and Kautilya's Arthashastra mention Charvakas as strong in arguments and proponents of the belief that everything is governed by natural laws. This suggests that Charvakas may have believed in more than just direct perception and were among the earliest proponents of logic in Indian philosophy.

Perception Is the Only Way

Indian philosophy is concerned with knowing the truth, knowing reality. Towards this end, it is in constant search of the source of such knowledge (*pramana*). For Charvakas, perception is the only source of dependable knowledge. Other schools of philosophy consider inference (deriving a new truth from a few observations or previous truths) and testimony (the perception of others) also as valid *pramanas*. But the Charvakas do not. They agree that inference is useful, but it can never be 100 per cent reliable.

Charvakas rely on external perception – which is acquired through the five senses, and internal perception – acquired through the mind.

The Charvaka position on perception being the only true source of knowledge can be illustrated through the famous example of fire and smoke. When someone witnesses a rising column of smoke in the forest, they cannot immediately conclude that a fire caused it. This amounts to inferring the presence of fire, which was unobserved from the presence of smoke that was observed. Such a jump from a perceived phenomenon to an unperceived phenomenon, which is inference, is not a valid source of knowledge. This inference may be justified by previous experience of noticing a fire whenever there is smoke. But from a few inferences, one cannot arrive at the truth that all instances of fire are accompanied by smoke. This can be declared as truth only if the person has observed all cases of fire and all cases of smoke in the past, present and future – which is an impossible task.

A causal relationship cannot be established between fire and smoke. No one can conclusively assert that all fires can cause smoke. There may be unperceived conditions in a causal relationship. For instance, there may be smoke from a fire only when the wood is wet. A causal relationship can have many conditions, and it may be impossible to observe all conditions through perception.

> **Did the Charvakas Believe Only in Perception?**
>
> Madhava's treatment of the Charvaka theory of knowledge would lead us to the belief that the Charvakas believed only in direct perception as a valid source of knowledge. But believing only in perception would make life impossible. For example, if one cannot infer that wherever there is smoke there is a fire, then it would be impossible to check each instance of smoke.
>
> However, various texts mention that Lokayatikas or Charvakas did have a positive attitude to logic and arguments.
>
> *Sukra Niti Sara* (a treatise on the science of governance) mentions nastikas, the Lokayatikas, as very strong in arguments. They denied god and the authority of the Vedas, but they also believed in *sarvam svabhavikam matam*, a doctrine according to which everything is governed by natural laws.
>
> Kautilya, in his treatise *Arthashastra*, called Saankhya, Yoga and Lokayata the science of logic, *anvikshiki*. Manu himself – though he called them heretics, hypocrites and transgressors of caste discipline – mentioned logic and logicians as associated with Lokayatikas.
>
> So it is quite possible that the Lokayatikas believed in more than direct perception as a valid source of knowledge and were also among the earliest logicians in Indian philosophy.
>
> Source: Chattopadhyay, D. *Lokayata*. pp. 22–30

Testimonials again pose problems. Hearing the testimony of an authoritative person is a valid perception because the sense of hearing is used. But if the words in the testimony of the authoritative person are not fully understood by the one who heard, then there are possibilities of errors and doubts. For example, the Charvakas pointed to how the priests chanting the Vedas were considered authoritative. But their words are meant to deceive the worshipper with false hopes that if they perform the rituals and sacrifices in the right way, then they can attain salvation. But it is the priests who actually gain from such rituals. We believe that expert advice is reliable. From that, we infer that all reliable authority gives expert advice, which is an inference, and hence, is not dependable.

Charvakas pose the question of passing from the particulars to the universal. At the same time, they accept that certain underlying phenomena of the world are universal, such as the hotness of a fire and the coolness of water in the river. These objects have a universal character because of their inherent nature (*svabhava*). Moreover, the inherent nature was not created by a supernatural force.

The positive aspect of Charvakas' outlook is that one has to be cautious about coming to conclusions from a few inferences or testimonies. Direct perception is the best way to confirm whether a relationship or a phenomenon is true or false.

Does a Soul Exist?

The Charvakas believe that the material world consists of four kinds of elements: i) air (*vayu*), fire (*agni*), water (*ap*) and earth (*ksiti*). Unlike other systems, they dismiss ether (*akasa*) as a fifth element because ether cannot be perceived. All living and non-living objects in the world are composed of these four elements. The living beings are reduced to these elements when they die.

The Charvakas do admit that living beings have consciousness but dismiss the idea that this consciousness is non-material or spiritual. Consciousness is perceivable, and it is nothing but the quality of the body itself. One perceives that one is tall or short, fat or lean. Therefore the self, the 'I' is a part of the body that does not have a different existence. The Charvakas assert that consciousness is produced by the four elements within a body interacting with each other as in a chemical reaction. For example, areca nut is folded into a betel leaf with a coating of white lime, and the compound becomes red when chewed. Molasses, when fermented, becomes an intoxicant. Similarly, consciousness is a product of matter interacting with each other.

The Charvakas argue that since we cannot perceive the soul, it does not exist, let alone have immortality. When the body dies,

Are Charvakas and Asuras the Same?

The Chandogya Upanishad, while relating the story of Indra and Virochana, says that those who are immersed in worldly pleasures, those who do not believe in the immortality of the soul and those who do not perform Vedic sacrifices are asuras (demons). The asuras dressed their dead in good clothes with ornaments and buried them along with food items in the belief that they would conquer the other world. The Charvakas, however, did not believe in the existence of another world. They declared that the body and the self are the same and with the death of the body, the self also disappears.

The Bhagavat Gita describes the asuras as those people who do not believe that the world is based on truth and reality; they do not believe in god and put sexual desires above all. They live an impure life and believe that their existence stops with death. Because of their unquenchable desires, they covet property and material goods.

Similarly, in the Ramayana, Jabali preaches a way of life similar to what the Lokayatas believe. He wonders how some people can prefer virtue in another world compared to the pleasures of this world. Also, he ridicules the custom of *shraddha*, the ritual of offering food for the dead, and sarcastically comments that if food eaten by one person could be transferred to another person in another world, then this can be useful for travellers visiting faraway places. They don't need to carry food!

Elsewhere in the Mahabharata, references are made to the haitukas, who were well-read in the Vedas and performed sacrifices and made gifts but did not believe in the existence of the other world or a permanent soul.

These references to Asuras and the views of Charvakas in the epics admit the differences and acrimony between Vedic and non-Vedic schools of thought and even within Vedic circles.

Refer: Dasgupta S., *A History of Indian Philosophy*, Vol. 1, pp. 767-805

Source: *A History of Indian Philosophy*, Vol 1, pp. 783–85

consciousness also dies. The body disintegrates and returns to the four elements. Therefore, there is no afterlife, and the cycle of birth and rebirth is utter nonsense. There is no such thing as karma from previous birth or reward or punishment for good or bad deeds in this life. All that matters is to live one's life in this world.

The soul cannot be perceived, and neither can god be perceived. How the four elements were created cannot be perceived either. But what matters is that once the four elements are present, then they combine according to their *svabhava* into different living and non-living beings. There is no need for a god to complete this chemical reaction since the elements combine according to their in-built nature. This leads the Charvakas to conclude that there is no creator or supreme being. There is no conscious purpose behind the functioning of the universe.

Live Your Life

Because the Charvakas dismissed life after death and advised their followers to live their lives fully in this world, they were called hedonists, pleasure-seekers. Their theories hurt the Brahmanical priests because they held the view that the priests duped the people by promising them a passage to heaven if they did their rituals properly and condemnation to hell if they didn't. While other schools of thought put liberation from the cycle of birth as the ultimate goal of life, the Charvakas argued that since there was no soul and no external worlds, one should minimize the pain of their existence in this world and maximize their pleasure. They stood in total opposition to asceticism. To them, pleasure-seeking was not a sin. Since our body will return to its elements after death, it only makes sense to enjoy the pleasures of this life as much as possible.

The portrayal of Charvakas as pleasure-seekers by other schools may not all be reliable. Since the Charvaka texts are extinct, what we get to know about them is through selected quotations from their works by their competitors, such as Buddhists, Jains and Brahmins.

Ajita Kesakambali

We witnessed a discussion between King Ajatashatru and proponents of the Ajivika school in a previous chapter as reported in the Buddhist text *Digha Nikaya*. The king also met Ajita and asked him the same question – whether leading a contemplative life would bear fruits in this life. Ajita replied:

> 'There is no such thing, O king, as alms or sacrifice or offering. There is neither fruit nor result of good or evil deeds. There is no such thing as this world or the next. There is neither father nor mother nor beings springing into life without them. There are in the world no recluses or *Brahmins* who have reached the highest point, who walk perfectly, and who having understood and realized, by themselves alone, both this world and the next, make their wisdom known to others.

> A human being is built up of the four elements. When he dies, the earthy in him returns and relapses to the earth, the fluid to the water, the heat to the fire, the windy to the air, and his faculties pass into space. The four bearers, on the bier as a fifth, take his dead body away; till they reach the burning ground, men utter forth eulogies, but there, his bones are bleached and his offerings end in ashes. It is a doctrine of fools, this talk of gifts. It is an empty lie, mere idle talk, when men say there is profit therein. Fools and wise alike, on the dissolution of the body, are cut off, annihilated, and after death, they are not.'

It is clear that Ajita's world outlook was similar to that of Gosala. He denied the existence of any external world. He did not believe in the cycle of birth, rebirth and karma. He detested Vedic sacrifices. According to him, the body was made up of the four elements and there was no separate soul. When the body died, it returned to the dust.

Key Takeaways

- The Charvaka school of philosophy, also called the Lokayata, relies on materialism as its world outlook.
- The adherents of this school rejected the existence of souls and the theory of transmigration. They refused to accept any reality other than what was perceived, and that included the existence of a supreme being.
- The primary document of the Charvakas has been mentioned in other sources as the Brihaspati Sutra, but this text has not survived.
- The only sources of the Charvaka school are Buddhist and Jain texts, which do not portray the Charvakas in a good light.
- They acknowledged the material human body and the material universe as the only reality.

- The Charvakas rely on external perception – which is acquired through the five senses, and internal perception – acquired through the mind.
- The Charvakas do admit that living beings have consciousness but dismiss the idea that this consciousness is non-material or spiritual.
- The Charvakas were called hedonists and pleasure-seekers by rival schools of thought.

Fact Check (Answers at the Back)

1. The Charvakas have a materialist philosophy as their world outlook. (Yes, No)
2. For the Charvakas, inference is a valid source of knowledge. (Yes, No)
3. The Charvakas were opposed to Vedic rituals and sacrifices. (Yes, No)
4. The Charvakas believed in a permanent soul and life after death. (Yes, No)
5. The opinion that the Charvakas were hedonists and pleasure-seekers may not be reliable. (Yes, No)
6. Lokayata means 'prevalent among the people'. (Yes, No)
7. The most important document of the Charvaka philosophy is the Brihaspati Sutra, which is now lost. (Yes, No)
8. Buddhists and Jain texts and the *Brahma Sutras* talk about the Charvakas in glowing terms. (Yes, No)

9

Saankhya and Yoga: Purusha and Prakriti

Kapila, the great sage, is believed to be the conceptualizer of the Saankhya system of thought. There are numerous references to this line of thought in the *srutis*, *smritis* and *puranas*, leading us to believe that it has very ancient roots in Indian thought. Kapila had first expounded the Saankhya thought in a terse book called the *Saankhya Sutra*. A later work by the same sage, called the *Saankhya Pravachana Sutra*, has a more elaborate discussion of the Saankhya philosophy. Like the other 'atheistic' philosophies of Buddhism and Jainism, Saankhya dismisses the existence of god. But there are many other aspects where it differs from the atheistic schools. The *Saankhya Karika* is an authoritative book on the later Saankhya school of philosophy.

> **Sage Kapila**
>
> Several Sanskrit texts refer to the name Kapila. There may have been many sages with this name. The most celebrated of them, however, is the sage Kapila who, along with his student Asuri, founded the Saankhya school of philosophy.
>
> Since the earliest Buddhist texts refer to him, it is generally assumed that he lived before the time of the Buddha, sometime in the sixth or seventh century BCE – the late Vedic period.
>
> Kapila authored the *Saankhya Sutra*, which has been lost.

There are several interpretations of the origin of the name 'Saankhya'. A simple explanation is that it means a number or a total. Since it has worked out an exhaustive list of objects of knowledge, the name may, after all, be appropriate. Like other systems, the Saankhya system also considers that emancipation, an end to all pain and suffering, is possible only when one attains knowledge of reality. One can find a brilliant exposition of the metaphysical description of the self. The system recognizes two kinds of ultimate realities, called the *purusha* (spirit) and *prakriti* (matter). In this, it differs from the Charvakas, who recognize only matter as reality and other systems like the Nyaya and Vaisheshika, which believe that there are many realities such as atoms, minds and souls.

How Do We Acquire Knowledge?

We saw earlier that the Charvakas considered only perception as the true source of knowledge. According to them, inference and testimony are not dependable sources of knowledge.

But the Saankhya school does not think so. Three sources of valid knowledge (*pramana*) are acceptable. They are *pratyaksha* (direct perception through the senses), *anumana* (inference) and *shabda* (testimony of authoritative seers and texts).

Perception can be both external and internal. External perception is possible through the recognition of objects using the five senses. Internal perception is through the mind.

When one uses inference to know the truth, then they acquire knowledge through a few observations or based on previous truths by applying reason. The Charvakas say that by observing smoke one cannot infer that a fire has caused it. The Saankhya school does not accept this stand. Inference is an important method of acquiring knowledge. It usually consists of three parts: i) a hypothesis or idea that must be proven or disproven,

ii) a reason advanced to prove the hypothesis and iii) positive examples as evidence and negative examples as counter-evidence justifying the reason. The reason must be sufficiently robust to prove the hypothesis in all cases.

The Saankhya school holds that it is not possible to observe all instances of a relation to prove a point. For example, it is not possible to observe all instances of fire and smoke in the universe to conclude that fire is accompanied by smoke. We have to use the method of inference but with sufficient conditionalities. In any case, even to recognize that we have sense organs, we need the method of inference. How do we know that we have the five senses? We do not have a special sense organ to perceive their existence. Therefore, to prove the existence of the senses, we have to take recourse to inference. We have to advance the reason that all action requires a means, that perception is an action, and therefore, it requires a means, and finally, that the five senses are the means to the action called perception.

The third method of acquiring knowledge according to the Saankhya school is by relying on testimony. In this universe of ever-expanding knowledge, it is not possible for a human being to know everything because life is finite and energy is limited. Therefore, we should not hesitate to gather knowledge from authoritative sources, both spoken and written. The Saankhya school dismisses testimony as a reliable source of information. Other schools are also concerned about reliability. They suggest various means to establish reliability. In the Saankhya school, testimonies of ordinary trustworthy individuals cannot be admitted as a reliable *pramana*. But the testimony of the Vedas (*srutis*) is reliable as the Vedas are sacred, infallible, universal and impersonal. So, the Saankhya school accepts the infallibility of the Vedas as opposed to the heterodox sects of Buddhism, Jainism, Charvakas and others who deny it.

How Was the World Created?

The Charvaka, Buddhist, Jain and Nyaya–Vaisheshika systems hold that the atoms of earth, ether, light and air constitute the material causes of the objects we see in the world.

The Saankhya system does not accept this view. It argues that certain intangible products of nature, such as the mind, ego, and intellect, could not have been produced by a combination of material atoms unless there was a subtle cause driving the production of these objects. For example, the seed is the cause of the tree and gets subsumed by the effect, which is the tree[1].

If this logic is extended to the creation of the world, then there must have been an ultimate cause that gave birth to the world and its various objects. The Saankhya system calls this *prakriti*, the first cause, which itself dialectically does not have a cause. It is very difficult to describe *prakriti* because it is subtle, eternal, ubiquitous and cannot be perceived. It is the cause of the beginning of the world as well as the end of the world. It is the force behind the cyclic nature of the universe, the coming and going of the universe and its objects.

The Charvakas dismissed the concept of *prakriti* because it cannot be perceived and any other method of knowing it, such as inference, is unreliable. The Saankhya system argues that since all objects of the universe are limited and non-eternal, there must be an unlimited, eternal cause that created them. All effects must have causes, and the effects acquire their potentialities, which already reside in the cause. The effect that arises from the cause disappears into it when it dies. From *prakriti*, energy is created, which in turn creates atoms, atoms into elements and elements into complex elements and objects. When the object is destroyed, the reverse takes place.

We find that various objects in the universe have different qualities, called *gunas*. There are three *gunas* – *sattva*, *rajas* and *tamas*. The *gunas* are intangible; they cannot be perceived. But they are manifest in various objects. It is only logical that when the effects, i.e., the objects of the world, have these elements, then the first cause, *prakriti*, should have also been made of these elements. At the beginning of the creation of the universe in a new cycle, these *gunas* are in a state of complete equilibrium. Once the *gunas* are disturbed by the contact of the *purusha* and *prakriti*, then there is no stopping them. From then on, the world is in a constant state of motion, with objects coming into being and disappearing continuously.

Sources of Saankhya

Saankhya is among the oldest philosophical systems.

One line of thought in the Upanishads defined the ultimate reality as Brahman, which was pure bliss and knowledge. It represented the power of sacrifices. It was the universal and supreme principle from which all other objects derived. This thought developed into the Advaita Vedanta of Shankara, which denied the reality of the world and concluded that the ultimate knowledge of the Brahman is the only truth.

Another line of thought developed parallelly, which believed that the world was made of water, fire and earth and was real. Svetaswara, Katha and Maitrayani Upanishads had passages using technical terms of the Saankhya philosophy.

Charaka, who lived in the fourth century BCE, has explained the Saankhya philosophy in a detailed manner in his *Charaka Samhita*.

The Mahabharata refers to an earlier school of Saankhya.

The *Saankhya Karika*, written by Ishwarakrishna in the third century CE, though a later work, is the oldest Saankhya text on which other scholars have written their commentaries. But it differs from the earlier school of Saankhya in its conception of a supreme being.

Sattva is an element that can be described as lightness, joy, illumination and poise. *Rajas* is mobile, stimulating, restless and painful. *Tamas* represents passivity, resistance, heaviness, laziness and indifference.

The three *gunas* are in constant conflict with each other. In fact, if they stop being in conflict, if they stop constantly changing, then the world will come to an end. This is the dialectic of the *gunas*. There is always tension between the three *gunas* as they try to dominate an object. An object is also classified in accordance with the preponderance of the *gunas*. An object can be good or bad, energetic or slothful, full of pain or pleasure depending on which *guna* dominates it. The *gunas* can create effects only when they work together. When the oil, wick and flame come together, then the lamp shines. A *guna* doesn't have an existence independent of the other two.

Saankhya

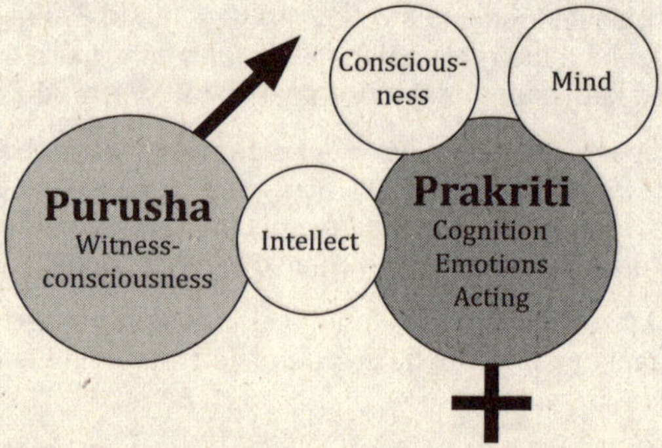

Purusha is 'witness-consciousness'. Undeterminable, inreducible, unobjectifiable, undestructible.

Prakriti includes all the cognitive, moral, psychological, emotional, sensorial and physical aspects of reality.

Figure 8: *Purusha-prakriti*

We saw that the Saankhya system considers *prakriti* as a type of ultimate reality. There is also another type of ultimate reality that Saankhya recognizes, and that is *purusha*. The *purusha* is nothing but the self, the 'I', the consciousness. It cannot be perceived, but it can be inferred because it is self-manifest; everyone can feel it. No one can deny its existence. For the Charvakas, the self, mind and consciousness are nothing different from the body itself; they are just forms of matter. Buddhists consider it as consciousness.

In Saankhya thought, the self has a different existence from the body, the senses, the mind (*manas*) and intellect (*buddhi*). The self is pure consciousness. It is not matter. It is not an object, it is not an effect of a cause. It is also not a cause. It is free from all the material aspects of the world, beyond pain and pleasure, beyond change and activity.

The Saankhya idea of the self is like the mechanic who makes a machine work or the driver who makes the car move. Only when material objects, mind and intellect are directed by a conscious principle can they be expected to serve a purpose.

The Saankhya system calls this self the *purusha*. Unlike the Vedanta system, which believes in one universal self pervading all bodies, the Saankhya system admits the plurality of selves.

The coming together of *purusha* and *prakriti* is the starting point of the evolution of the world. It is their contact that triggers *prakriti* to cause all the objects of the universe. The inactive *purusha* and the non-intelligent *prakriti* cannot act on their own to evolve the universe. They need each other like the blind man and the lame man who help each other to find their way out of a forest. But the contact between *purusha* and *prakriti* is not any kind of contact that two material objects can have. *Purusha* moves *prakriti* similar to how a thought moves a person to act.

Their coming into contact also upsets the balance of the *gunas* in the universe. Before creation, the *gunas* are perfectly balanced, a state in which there is no motion and an absence of senses.

Once the equilibrium of the *gunas* is disturbed by the coming together of *purusha* and *prakriti*, the balance among the *gunas* is destroyed. The contention between the *gunas* to dominate each other results in the creation of the objects of the world.

Saankhya philosophy goes to great lengths on how the evolution of *prakriti* takes place. The first product of evolution is intellect (*mahat* or *buddhi*). *Mahat*, meaning 'the great one', is the great germ of world objects. In individual beings, it is called *buddhi* or intellect. It is the intellect that is responsible for ascertaining various objects and for decision-making. Among the *gunas*, it has a preponderance of sattva. Next in the evolutionary process comes the ego (*ahankara*). It is responsible for generating the feeling of 'I' and 'mine'. It is this principle that binds the self to the material world.

The predominance of *sattva* in *ahankara* gives rise to five organs of perception, five organs of action and the mind (*manas*) itself. The predominance of *tamas* in *ahankara* gives rise to five subtle elements called *tanmatras*. The gross physical elements (*mahabhutas*) arise from the *tanmatras*, providing a gross element for the expression of each of the subtle senses.

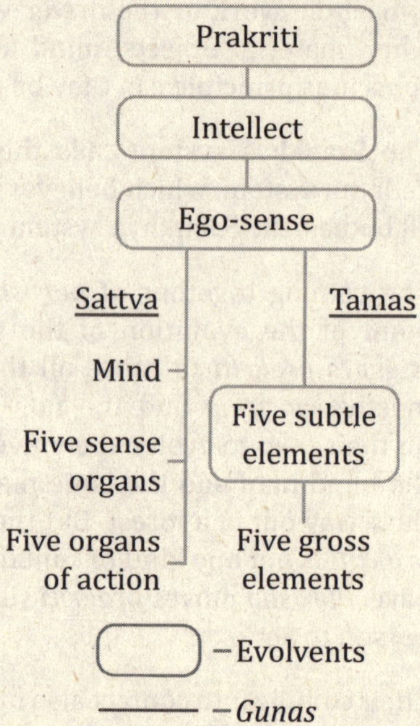

Figure 9: *Evolution of prakriti*

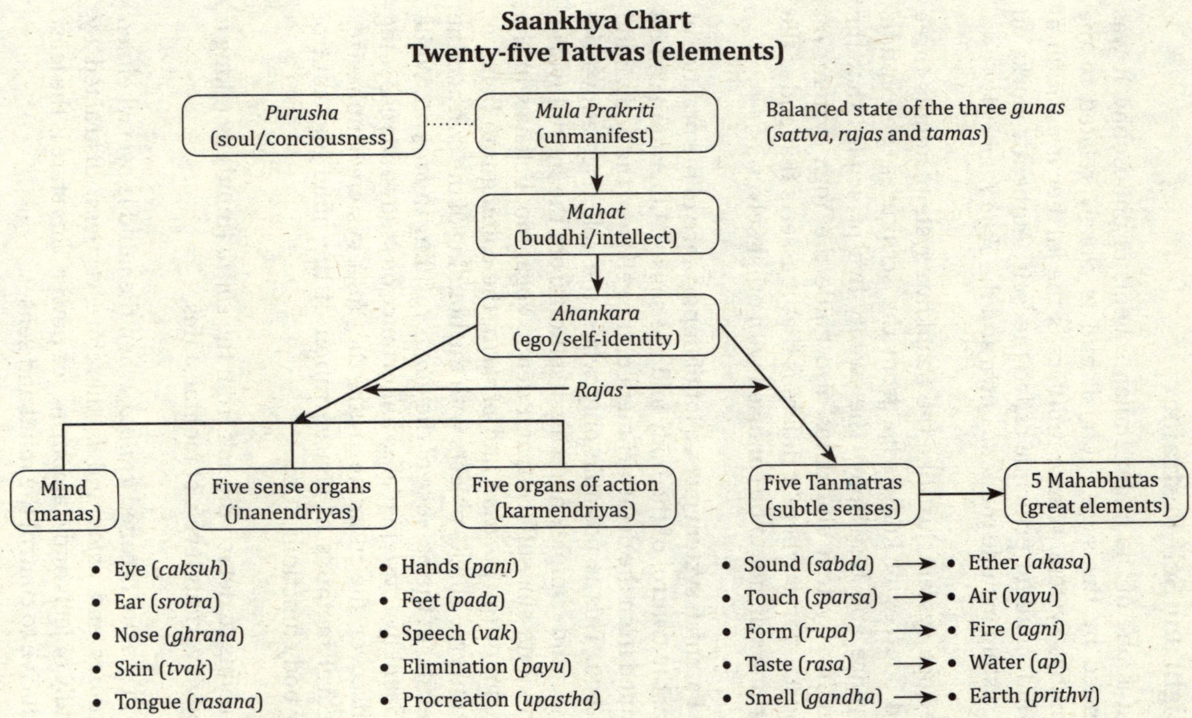

Figure 10: *Saankhya philosophy - 24 principles*

Insight and Self-Restraint

Yoga is one of the major Indian schools of philosophy. It was founded by the sage Patanjali and is closely related to the Saankhya system. Where it differs is the further exposition of the independent principle called the 'self'. Authentic works on the system include the *Yoga Sutra* and the *Yoga Bhashya*.

The Yoga system, just like the Saankhya system, admits three valid sources of knowledge from the scriptures: perception, inference and testimony. The twenty-five principles that the Saankhya system elucidates also guide the Yoga system. An important area where it differs is that it asserts that god is the supreme self, not to be confused with other selves.

The Patanjali system gives a lot of importance to the practice of Yoga, the control of the body and the senses. Liberation can be attained from the de-attachment of the self from the body, mind and ego. This is possible only when the self rises above the body–mind complex and cuts itself off from the mortal world, with all its sin, suffering and death. Yoga, too, believes in the dualism of the *purusha* and *prakriti*, the coming into being of the universe and its objects with the bonding of the two and the upsetting of the balance of the *gunas* residing in *prakriti*. While the Saankhya system places importance on study and reasoning to discover the ultimate truth, the Yoga system emphasizes practical methods of concentration of the mind and control over body functions.

Yoga aims to detach the self from the *chitta* (mind) by taking it through various levels of mental states.

The first state is called *kshipta*, when the mind is overwhelmed by *tamas* and *rajas* and is therefore restless, distracted by worldly objects and clamouring for power. This state is the least conducive to control the mind and senses.

In the second stage, called *mudha*, the mind is dominated by *tamas*, thus making it slothful, ignorant and filled with vice.

In the third stage, called *vikshipta*, the mind is fairly free of the domination of *tamas*, open to acquiring virtue and knowledge, but distracted.

In the fourth stage, called *ekagra*, the mind is purged of *tamas* and *rajas* and comes under the sway of *sattva*, thus making it capable of concentration and preparing conditions for the weeding out of all mental turbulence.

In the final stage, *niruddha*, all mental activities cease, and the mind attains its original state of balance and tranquillity.

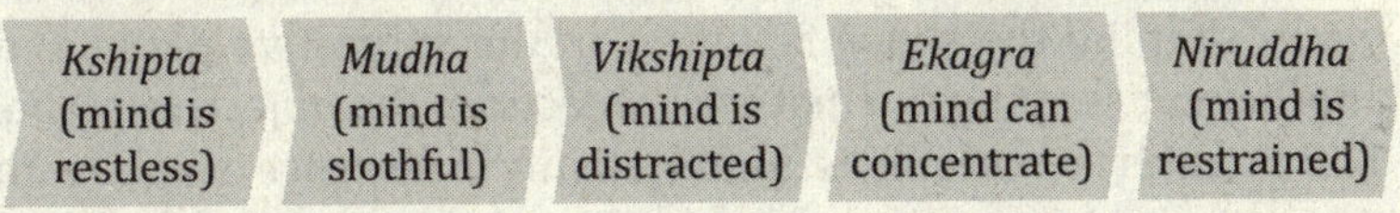

Figure 11: *Various mental states of Yoga*

For the purification and enlightenment of the mind, Yoga advocates eight disciplines, as shown below, which need to be practised regularly.

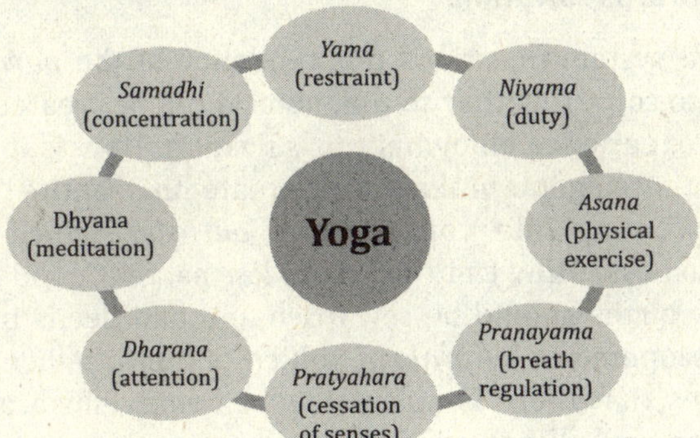

Figure 12: *The eight disciplines of Yoga*

Was the Universe Created by an Intelligent Being?

The Saankhya system holds that at the beginning of the universe, the *purusha* and *prakriti* are in a state of equilibrium, changeless and motionless. This is the state of *pralaya* (a dormant state). What causes the first imbalance that connects the *purusha* to *prakriti* and sets in motion the creation of objects and all the effects we see in the real world? Saankhya tries to answer this knotty question, but it denies the existence of an omniscient super being, the Ishwara (god) or for that matter any other external influence. It explains the logic of the automatic movement of the *purusha* towards *prakriti* by the argument that the selves always strive to go in the direction of enjoyment or salvation, which is a liberation from enjoyment. Accordingly, the *gunas* are set in motion, one combination of *gunas* shaping the sense faculties on the subjective plane and another set shaping the material objects on the objective plane. The Saankhya outlook is materialistic in essence since both thought and matter are objects of *prakriti*, made of material substances, the only difference being the proportion of *gunas* constituting them. This is the tendency of the self that results in the creation of a world of objects and experiences. It is also the same tendency that draws the self away from the materialistic world towards salvation.

The Yoga system questions this tendency of the *purusha* and *prakriti* to come together so that objects can be created and the self can experience enjoyment or salvation. How is it possible that non-intelligent *prakriti* can create this entire universe just by coming into contact with *purusha*, which is pure consciousness? How can the law of karma, that good deeds in previous births should be rewarded and bad deeds punished, be made operative by *prakriti*, which is non-intelligent? Yoga postulates that there is an intelligent being, Ishwara, who is omniscient and all-powerful. This being does not create *prakriti* but only disturbs the equilibrium of *prakriti* in its dormant state and then guides it to create a world of harmony and purpose.

Is Saankhya Non-Vedic?

According to the classical tradition of categorizing schools of philosophy into astika and nastika schools, only Buddhist, Jain and Charvaka schools are generally considered as nastika schools – heterodox schools that reject Vedic orthodoxy. The Saankhya school is normally considered an astika school.

> **The *Brahma Sutra* of Badarayana, which attempted to systematize the philosophy of the Upanishads, termed Saankhya philosophy as non-Vedic.**

According to the Brahma Sutra, the realization of truth cannot be achieved through independent reasoning. The knowledge is already revealed in the Vedas (the srutis), and therefore, cannot be reinvented. This goes against the Saankhya theory of *prakriti* being the source of knowledge when it becomes active in contact with the *purusha*. There are sixty aphorisms in the Brahma Sutra that argue against the premises of Saankhya philosophy. Of these, thirty-seven aphorisms try to prove the anti-Vedic nature of Saankhya.

Saankhya says that it is unconscious *prakriti* when it comes into contact with the conscious *purusha* that becomes the first cause of the material world. The Upanishads, however, argue that the first cause is the Brahman, the spiritual principle.

The Brahma Sutra tries to establish that Saankhya is not supported by srutis. Not only that, the Saankhya Sutra of Kapila cannot even be accepted as a part of the smritis .

The Early Saankhya System

Saankhya philosophy has influenced Indian thought so much that from the Mahabharata to the Manu Smriti and the Puranas, there are extensive references to this doctrine.

Even Shankara, the greatest exponent of the Vedanta school of philosophy, who wrote critically about the Saankhya system, admitted that it had weighty arguments and had the backing of several eminently wise men.

Despite this, genuinely authentic materials on the original Saankhya philosophy are hard to come by. There is no authentic proof that Kapila was the founder of the system. Neither is there clarity on the meaning of the name Saankhya.

Two texts are attributed to the Saankhya system, the *Saankhya Karika* and the *Saankhya Sutra*.

Ishwara Krishna's *Saankhya Karika* is one of the oldest surviving works of the Saankhya school. There are many commentaries on the *Saankhya Karika*, such as Gaudapada's *Bhashya*, Vachaspati Mishra's *Tattva Kaumudi*, Narayana Tirtha's *Samkhya Chandrika* and the *Yuktidipika*.

There is a collection of Saankhya texts called the *Saankhya Pravachana Sutra*, which is of a much later date, around the fourteenth century CE, and hence, cannot be accepted as an original Saankhya document.

It is believed that the later renditions of the Saankhya doctrine took it closer to the Vedanta school, while the original Saankhya outlook dismissed the idea of the world being created by a supreme god. As Richard Garbe, a well-known commentator on Saankhya philosophy, put it:

> Even in the Saankhya Sutra themselves… the Saankhya doctrine no longer appears in its original unadulterated form; for they seek to explain away the points of discrepancy between themselves on the one hand and the teachings of the Upanishads and the Vedanta on the other. In particular, the author of the sutras is at great pains to furnish proof

of the utterly impossible thesis that the teachings of the Saankhya system are not in irreconcilable contradiction with the doctrine of personal god, with the doctrine of the all-embracing unity of Brahman, with the doctrine of the nature of the Brahman as bliss (*ananda*), and with the doctrine of the attainment of the highest aim in the heavenly world[2].

The *Saankhya Karika* attributed to Ishwarakrishna is dated between the second and fifth centuries CE. It is a set of seventy cryptic aphorisms that can only be understood by reading commentaries on them, such as Anirudha's and Vachaspi Mishra's.

The oldest Saankhya texts have been lost but from quotes in the Mahabharata and Arthashastra, it can be presumed that Saankhya is among the oldest systems of Indian philosophy, probably even earlier than Buddhism.

Perhaps the original Saankhya could be better understood by the criticism of it in the Brahma Sutra, which is dated around the second century BCE. It could be even earlier because of many earlier preparatory texts on the sutra[3].

Idealism and Materialism in Indian Thought

The debate between idealism and materialism has a long history in Indian thought. Indian philosophers have been divided between the *pradhana karana vada* (the doctrine of pradhana being the first cause, the ultimate reality) and *Brahma karana vada* (the doctrine according to which Brahman is the first cause, the ultimate reality). Pradhana means *prakriti* in Saankhya terms. *Prakriti* is the non-intelligent primeval matter which, when it comes into contact with the *purusha*, becomes active. The *purusha*, as we have seen, hardly has a role in the creation and motion of the universe.

In the Brahma Sutra, the author Badarayana explains that the Brahman of the Vedanta is different from the pradhana of the Saankhya. Brahman was an intelligent principle while pradhana of the Saankhya was non-intelligent.

To look at it from another angle, the tussle between the *Brahma karana vada* and *pradhana karana vada* was actually the conflict between *chetana vada* (the doctrine of consciousness being the first cause) and *achetana vada* (unconscious matter being the first cause).

While they had their own differences, both Shankara and Ramanuja opposed the Saankhya doctrine. In the words of Ramanuja:

> The sutra (Brahma Sutra) means to say that by the demolition given above (in the Brahma Sutra) of the Saankhya doctrine which is not comprised within the Veda, the remaining theories which are in the same position, namely the theories of Kanada, Akshapada, Jina and the Buddha, must likewise be considered as demolished.

Saankhya and Yoga

The meaning of Yoga is yoking or harnessing. It also means certain exercises that help one to attain the highest spiritual level. Yoga is connected to the Saankhya philosophy, except for the introduction of the concept of god in the latter.

It is quite possible that in the early stages, there was one composite system incorporating the theoretical and practical viewpoints of both the systems, the primordial nature of reality. It is only later that Saankhya emerged as a theoretical system and Yoga as a practical one. When idealistic notions were introduced into the later Saankhya, there is reason to believe that the same process happened to Yoga as well. The Yoga Sutra of Patanjali reflects the later stages of the Yoga school of philosophy.

Interpretation of the Soul or Self across Schools of Philosophy

Saankhya	Jain	Buddhism	Charvaka	Advaita Vedanta
The Saankhya system says there are two ultimate realities – *purusha* (soul) and *prakriti* (matter). Souls are many. They are not contained in the bodies. They are all-pervasive. But the soul and mind are related in the sense that all mental phenomena happening in the mind are interpreted as the experience of the soul. Souls are characterized by absolute consciousness.	Souls (*jiva*) are many. They have consciousness as their essence. They differ according to the degree of consciousness. The soul is eternal, but it also undergoes changes. It is the soul that enables a living being to carry out activities and also experience pleasure, pain and other emotions. It exists independent of the body. The soul pervades the entire body. It can be directly perceived by anyone just as they perceive any external object. To start with, the soul is in its pure state, but over many cycles of birth and rebirth, the soul gets tarnished by karma.	All phenomena have a conditional existence, and hence, cannot be real. This applies to the self also. The sense of permanence of the soul is our own belief and not a reality. What we call self is actually made up of a package of thoughts, feelings and beliefs that shows up at a particular moment and then vanishes. The next moment, a similar package appears, but it is not the same as the previous one. These momentary pictures come one after another in fast succession and resemble each other so much that it gives us a feeling of permanency.	All living and non-living objects in the world are composed of only four elements – air, fire, water and earth. Living beings are reduced to these elements when they die. Living beings have consciousness, but this consciousness is non-material or non-spiritual. Consciousness is perceivable, and it is nothing but the quality of the body itself.	Individual souls are mere manifestations of the universal soul, the Brahman, which is pure consciousness. Souls are characterized by pure intelligence and bliss.

Liberation from Sorrow

Saankhya, Yoga and Buddhism have similar views regarding the nature of all experiences being filled with sorrow. Intellectual operations involve some level of painful feelings, and even moments of pleasure are overshadowed by previous sorrows and the fear of losing that pleasure. The overall message of these schools is that the accumulation of sorrows outweighs the pleasures in life. They emphasize that temporary pleasures do not eradicate the roots of sorrow and that true liberation (*mukti*) from pain can only be achieved by understanding and accepting that all experiences are inherently sorrowful. They encourage individuals to turn away from worldly and heavenly pleasures, understanding that pursuing pleasures cannot ultimately eliminate sorrow.

> **It is important to recognize the existence of sorrow in all facets of life and seek philosophical understanding as a means to uproot it.**

Saankhya believes that to eradicate sorrow the mind (*chitta*) must be separated from the self (*purusha*) to end suffering. By developing a true understanding of the self in the mind, one can detach the mind from the self, leading to the destruction of ignorance. This separation allows the self to remain in its true form and achieve liberation. When the mind turns away from the self and stops binding it to sorrowful experiences, the self can attain freedom. Once this true knowledge arises, the cycle of experiences controlled by the material world (*prakriti*) ceases, fulfilling its final purpose for that individual. This knowledge allows the self to break free from bondage while others continue their cyclic experiences.

Yoga, however, asserts that mere philosophy is not enough for liberation. Simply having true knowledge to differentiate between self (*purusha*) and mind (*buddhi*) is insufficient. In Yoga, it is essential to completely eradicate all old habits and experiences stored in the mind so that they never resurface. When the mind is purified from all past conditioning, it reflects the true nature of the self, leading to a state of oneness. In this state, where all past conditioning and ignorance are eliminated, the mind can no longer cling to the self, and it returns to the material world (*prakriti*) like a stone falling from a mountaintop.

To eliminate these old habits effectively, it is necessary to follow a gradual process of practice. This practice involves adhering to higher moral standards, refining the mind and gradually shedding the habits of ordinary life. As the practitioner progresses, they need to continually improve and let go of even good practices to attain better ones. By advancing in this manner, the mind reaches its utmost purity and perfection, ultimately taking on the form of the self, leading to final liberation.

Key Takeaways

- Kapila, the great sage, is believed to be the conceptualizer of the Saankhya system of thought.
- The system recognizes two kinds of ultimate realities, called the *purusha* (spirit) and *prakriti* (matter). In this, it differs from the Charvakas, who recognize only matter as reality and other systems like the Nyaya and Vaisheshika, which believe that there are many realities such as atoms, minds and souls.
- The Saankhya system explains that *prakriti* is blind and unintelligent, and as such, is incapable of creating a world with a purpose on its own. Therefore, the *purusha*, which is nothing but the plurality of selves, intelligent itself but inactive and unchanging, is required to make *prakriti* act.
- The three valid sources of knowledge are *pratyaksha* (direct perception through the senses), *anumana* (inference) and *shabda* (testimony of authoritative seers and texts).
- Various objects in the universe have different qualities, called *gunas*. There are three *gunas* – *sattva*, *rajas* and *tamas*.

- The Brahma Sutra of Badarayana, which attempted to systematize the philosophy of the Upanishads, termed Saankhya philosophy as non-Vedic.
- The system has been criticized for various shortcomings. The act of coming into contact of the *purusha* and *prakriti* is not elaborated well in the system. How an intelligent principle is not able to act and is required to trigger an unintelligent principle that can act and change is not clear.
- The Yoga system of philosophy is one of the major Indian schools of philosophy. It was founded by the sage Patanjali and is closely related to the Saankhya system.
- Yoga aims to detach the self from the *chitta* (mind) by taking it through five levels of mental states.

Fact Check (Answers at the Back)

1. Both the Lokayata and Saankhya systems believe that direct perception is the only valid source of knowledge. (Yes, No)
2. In the Saankhya system, the *purusha* and *prakriti* are ultimate realities. (Yes, No)
3. The Saankhya and Yoga systems of philosophy have diametrically opposite views. (Yes, No)
4. The Yogas system was founded by Kapila. (Yes, No).
5. The views of the earlier Saankhya system differed from those of the later Saankhya system. (Yes, No)
6. With the practice of Yoga, one can easily detach the self from the chitta (mind). (Yes, No)

10

Nyaya: Rational, Coherent Inquiry

One school of thought that gives primary importance to the acquiring of true knowledge of reality and the conditions required to achieve that is the Nyaya system of philosophy. It aims to inculcate the powers of logical reasoning and a rigorous, critical approach in its students. Therefore, the system is also known by other names such as Tarkashastra (the science of reasoning) and Anvikshiki (the science of critical inquiry). The school was founded by Aksapada Gautama, the author of the *Nyaya Sutras*.

Timelines of

Nyaya

Gautama Akshapada and the *Nyaya Sutras*—between the sixth century BC and the second century CE

Commentaries on the *sutras*:

- **5th–6th century** CE — *Pakṣilasvāmin Vātsyāyana*
- **6th–7th century** CE — *Nyāyavārttika* of Uddyotakāra
- **9th century** CE — Vācaspati Miśra's *Tatparyatika*
- **10th century** CE — Udayana's *Tātparyapariśuddhi*
- **10th century** CE — Jayanta's *Nyāyamañjarī*

But the system, while stressing on the search for true knowledge and the method of critical inquiry to pursue that goal, does not lose sight of the ultimate purpose of true knowledge. The system believes that true knowledge is the key to liberation, the ultimate release from *samsara*, the pain and suffering of material existence. If knowledge does not serve this purpose, then it is not of much use. In this aspect, the Nyaya school is not very different from many other schools. Where it differs from other schools is the method it advocates, the deployment of valid means of acquiring knowledge and developing a system of logic and critical inquiry in consummating that process.

The idea of using logic and critical reasoning goes back to Rig Vedic times. The pursuit of valid knowledge and the science of reasoning is reflected in the thoughts of Indian scholars as far back as the early centuries before the Common Era. However, it was only in the second century CE that Gautama Aksapada, the founder of the Nyaya system, laid down clear guidelines in the *Nyaya Sutra*. Later scholars refined the text and also introduced questions of a spiritual nature.

What Are Reliable Methods to Acquire True Knowledge?

The treatises that the Nyaya school developed on epistemology – the philosophical study concerned with the nature, source and limits of human knowledge – have influenced many other schools of Indian thought to no lesser degree.

We had seen earlier that the Charvakas considered that direct perception was the only means of *pramana*, the means of valid knowledge. The Saankhya system went one step further and

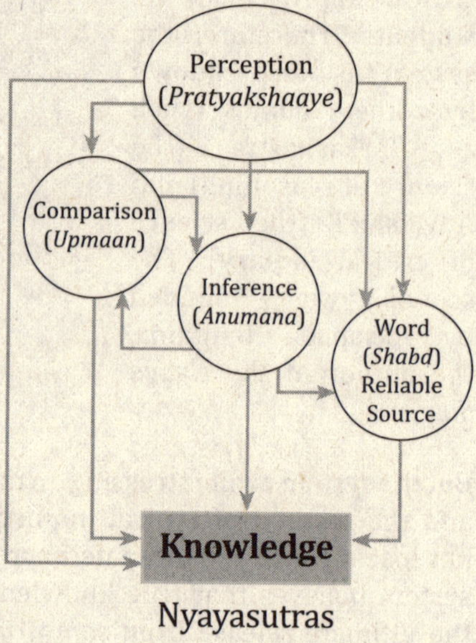

***Figure 13:** Valid means of knowledge – the Nyaya system of philosophy*

affirmed that perception, inference and testimony are all valid sources of knowledge. The Nyaya school expands the scope of *pramana* further by including a fourth source of knowledge, *upamana*, which means comparison.

The *Naiyayikas* (*Nyaya* scholars) accepted four means of obtaining valid knowledge (*pramana*) – perception (*pratyaksha*), inference (*anumana*), comparison (*upamana*) and testimony of reliable sources (*shabda*). The Nyaya scholars, along with those of other *darshana*s, also developed a theory of error. This theory outlines the means to identify errors, as well as the process by which errors are made in the acquiring of knowledge.

In the pursuit of knowledge, one can encounter doubts and inconsistencies (*samshaya*) as well as contrariness (*viparaya*). Nyaya outlines how these can be resolved or corrected using a systematic process of reasoning (*tarka*).

Philosophical Topics of the Nyaya System

SIXTEEN DIVISIONS (PADARTHAS) OF EXTERNAL REALITY

Nyaya divides perceivable and imperceivable reality into sixteen divisions (*padarthas*) that are:

- *Pramana*, the sources of knowledge
- *Prameya*, the object of knowledge
- *Samsaya*, doubt or the state of uncertainty
- *Prayojana*, the aim
- *Drstanta*, example
- *Siddhanta*, doctrine
- *Ayayava*, the constituents of inference
- *Tarka*, hypothetical argument
- *Nirnaya*, conclusion
- *Badha*, discussion
- *Jalpa*, wrangling
- *Vitanda*, irrational argument
- *Hervachasa*, specious reasoning
- *Chala*, unfair reply
- *Jati*, generality based on a false analogy
- *Nigrahsthana*, the grounds for defeat

Figure 14: *Philosophical topics of the Nyaya system*

To understand the Nyaya system in its entirety, we have to assimilate the sixteen philosophical topics (*padartha*) that make up the system.

The first one, *pramana*, as we have seen in the previous section, is the way to obtaining true knowledge. The Nyaya system considers perception, inference, testimony and comparison as the four valid means of *pramana*.

While *pramana* represents a valid means of obtaining true knowledge, the second philosophical topic of the Nyaya system, called *prameya*, represents the objects of valid knowledge. Such objects are the self, the body, senses, objects of the senses, cognition, mind, activity, mental defects, rebirth, suffering, and finally, liberation.

The third topic is *samshaya*, which represents the state of uncertainty, wavering and doubt. For instance, when we see an object at a distance, we are not sure whether it is a man or a pillar. The observation cannot be classified as certain, uncertain or an error. It is a state of temporary uncertainty where two mutually exclusive objects are occupying the same place at the same time.

The fourth, *prayojana*, denotes the end purpose of our activities, which may be to attain a desirable object or avert an undesirable object.

Drishtana, the fifth topic, represents an example of something that cannot be disputed, and therefore, can be made into a general rule. It is an apparent truth on which both parties of a debate agree upon. For instance, to make a general rule that there is smoke where there is fire, an example can be provided of smoke created by a lighted stove in the kitchen.

The sixth is *siddhanta*, a conclusion or tenet that is the underlying premise in a system of philosophy. For example, the Nyaya system accepts that there are four means of acquiring valid knowledge. This is an example of *siddhanta*.

While Nyaya accepts inference as a source of true knowledge, to meet the requirements of conclusive proof, it must be expressed in the form of five propositions, called the *avayavas* or members (see box).

Illustration of the Five-Membered Syllogism (*Avayava*) in Nyaya

1. Sita is a mortal (*pratignya* – proposition)
2. Because she is a woman (*hetu* – reason)
3. All women are mortal, e.g., Kaikeyi, Mandodhari (*udaharanam* – example)
4. Sita is also a woman (*upanayah* – application);
5. Therefore, she is a mortal (*nigamanam* – conclusion)

The next is *tarka*, hypothetical argument or reasoning, which justifies a certain premise by proving the non-validity of its opposite.

If one were to verify the truth about an object or a phenomenon by deploying recognized methods of validating knowledge, then that is *nirnaya*, the acquiring of certain knowledge.

The next topic in the Nyaya system is *vada*, where the person putting forward a view (*vadi*) and the person refuting it (*prativadi*) debate with each other using valid methods and hypothetical arguments to arrive at the truth. There are many instances when sages belonging to different systems of philosophy have debated with each other to arrive at the ultimate truth.

On the other hand, *jalpa* is mere squabbling between opponents without any intention of arriving at the truth. Their sole purpose is to defend their position.

In the method of *vithanda*, the debaters concentrate their energy on defeating the viewpoint of the opponents rather than establishing their own viewpoints. It is similar to *jalpa*, the difference being that this method justifies destructive criticism.

The next three topics, *hetvabhasha*, *chala* and *jati* represent fallacious arguments, quibbling, unfair responses, misrepresentation and so on.

The sixteenth topic, *nigrahasthana*, identifies grounds for defeat in a debate, such as misunderstanding the opponent's position or being incapable of understanding.

Was the Pot Already in the Clay?

Buddhism had given a jolt to beliefs in other schools of thought concerning substances and their qualities, cause and effect and the permanence of objects. The doctrine of momentariness of Buddhism (see the chapter on Buddhism) states that what we see of objects in the external world are just momentary instances and there is no permanence about them. Nyaya does not agree with this doctrine.

Nyaya argues that according to the doctrine of momentariness, even though white milk turns into white curd, the elements that constituted the composite thing called milk or curd had only momentary existences, and therefore, no continuity in substances or their qualities can be assumed. This goes against our normal experience. The qualities of clay get transferred to the pot when the potter turns the wheel.

If a cause that is supposed to create an effect is itself momentary, then how can it produce the effect? The elements constituting the cause require some time to create the conditions when they can come together and produce the effect. So, if the cause itself is momentary, how can the effect be produced? There needs to be continuity between the past, present and future for the cycle of cause and effect to persist. This is Nyaya's argument.

Nyaya is also merciless in its criticism of the Saankhya outlook. Saankhya assumes that a cause contains within it the effects that it would produce at a later time. The effect is in a potential state residing in the womb of the cause when it is not yet produced. Once it is produced, it enters a manifested state. Nyaya says that this logic is baseless. For instance, if sesame seed contains oil in a potential state, then why is a stone required to bring it out? Saankhya says that the stone is only an instrument to bring out the effect. Nyaya argues that if it were so, how can clay be confused with a pot, saying that the clay contains the jug in a potential state? Can clay hold water? Only when a potter with a wheel works on the clay, does it become a pot. So the pot was non-existent before. The clay indeed has within it the potency to become a pot under the hands of the potter. But this is not the same as saying that the pot was already in the clay as an unmanifested effect.

Nyaya also does not accept the Saankhya position that *buddhi* (consciousness) is non-intelligent. Nyaya believes that the soul feels, knows and has the capacity to will. Nyaya dismisses the double-reflection theory of Saankhya, where the consciousness of buddhi is reflected on the *purusha* and then back again on *buddhi*.

Mimansa believes that a particular cause produces a particular effect because it has some magical power within it. Nyaya denies this and explains that this can neither be proved by observation nor inference. Cause and effect are not a mystery, and they can be explained by molecular combination. The whole phenomenon involves molecular motion and redistribution of energy.

Soul, Ishwara and Salvation

One section of the Charvakas denied the existence of the soul altogether. For them, consciousness and life were just products of material changes. Another section believed there was a soul, which was different from the material body, but it did not have an existence beyond the body. The Buddhists also denied the existence of a permanent self.

The Naiyayikas differed from the above schools in their view of the soul. They inferred that things that cannot be felt by our senses, such as consciousness, pleasure and pain, belonged to another entity called the self. Since the self cannot be seen, its existence can only be inferred. But since nobody has witnessed the production or destruction of the *atman* (soul), it must be eternal. It is not located in any part of the body, but it can move the body and its sense organs through its will. To start with, it is unconscious but later acquires consciousness.

> **Nyaya believes that the inequalities in the world are due to one's karma in their past lives. The soul carries the memories of past actions and acts as a bridge between the past and present.**

In the same manner, using inference, Nyaya tries to establish the presence of a god who is the cause of the universe. In this, Nyaya differs fundamentally from Buddhist, Jain and Charvaka philosophy, which have no place for a god. Nyaya argues that just because we don't see the creator of a seed from which a tree grows, it doesn't mean that a creator doesn't exist. Everything that exists, like the jug or the universe, would have a creator. Just as our selves move the body and senses, so god wills the universe though he has no body. Nyaya believes that our bondage starts with the confusing of the self with the body, its ego and senses. Once a person attains full knowledge of the six padarthas and the sixteen categories, his ignorance is destroyed and he attains salvation. In Nyaya, salvation is not a state of bliss but a passive state that cannot feel pain or pleasure .

Is There an Intelligent Agent Who Created the World?

The Nyaya–Vaisheshika schools, being logic-oriented schools, developed a host of arguments to prove the existence of an intelligent creator, god. The school believed in the existence of a supreme, eternal, omniscient god.

On the other hand, Jainism did not believe that god is the creator and ruler of the world. They believed in the existence of many gods, but not eternal ones. The Jain gods are just embodied souls, like human beings and animals, but these souls have achieved a higher stage.

The table below illustrates the arguments of the two schools on this question.

Nyaya	Jainism
The world is of the nature of an effect. Some cause, an intelligent agent, must have created it.	If the world is an effect, then its parts must be destructible. But Nyaya regards the parts, such as *akasa*, as eternal. If the world is an effect because 'it was non-existent' before, then that is not true since Nyaya regards atoms making up the world as eternal. If the world is an effect because everyone regards it 'as being made', then even when man digs the ground and creates a hollow space, it can be treated as creation. If effect means that 'which is liable to change', then god was also liable to change because his creative ability needs to change.

The world was created by an intelligent cause.	Even if one agrees that the world is an effect of a creator, then the creator can also be as imperfect as human beings, who are also creators.
The world was created by a bodiless agent.	We have never so far seen such an agent without a body. Without a body, no physical movement is possible. If you observe a shoot of corn, you can see that no intelligent agent is producing the shoot.
God is abstract.	If an abstract creator is accepted, then it is possible to say that the world was created by an abstract potter, for example.
God created the world due to his will, activity or personal whim.	Then there can be no natural laws in the world. Since humans have a moral order, god must also have a moral order. If he created the world out of love for human beings, then there should have been only happiness.
Men suffer happiness or pain according to their past actions.	This is blind destiny. There is no need for a god for this.
God took to creation as mere play (*leela*).	Then he is like a child who does things without a purpose.
God is omniscient.	How can a being without a body and senses know everything?

The Nyaya Sutras

The *Nyaya Sutras* composed by Aksapada Gautama form the foundation of the Nyaya school of philosophy. The date of composition of the sutras is not clear. Some scholars estimate it to be around the sixth century BCE, the time when the Buddha and Mahavira lived. Others estimate it as late as the second century CE. It is also possible that the text may have been composed by multiple authors over centuries. The *Nyaya Sutras* are made up of five books, each book having two chapters. The entire work consists of 528 aphoristic sutras dealing with various topics, such as rules governing reason, basic rules of logic, an account of reliable sources of knowledge and questions relating to the origin of the universe, cause and effect, the soul, the nature of the supreme being, and others.

The *Nyaya Sutras* also expound *tarka vidya* (the science of debate) and *vada vidya* (the science of discussion). Later commentators like Pakshilaswamin, Uddyotakara, Vachaspi Mishra and Udayana discussed the sutras in depth.

Scholars believe that the sutras were not written in one time period or by one author. Books 1 and 5 may have been the earliest. Books 2 and 3 may have been written later. Ancient Buddhist texts make several references to the sutras.

Debates in Ancient India

There has been a long tradition of formal debates between proponents of various schools of thought in India. The debates were sometimes conducted under royal patronage in the assembly of kings, where philosophers from various corners of the subcontinent participated. The science of conducting debates in an organized fashion was called *vada vidya*. There is a significant corpus of literature describing the rules and ethical principles of conducting and taking part in these debates.

Though debates were popular from Vedic times, the theory of debates was not systematically penned until Buddhism and Jainism appeared on the scene. As early as the third century BCE, monks were required to become proficient in debating. However, some of the earliest manuals on debating have been lost.

The earliest formal document on the method of conducting debates is the *Charaka Samhita* (see the chapter on Ayurveda philosophy). The *Nyaya Sutra* further systematized the theory of debating. A philosophical debate is referred to as *katha* in Nyaya texts.

The Vaisheshika Philosophy

A closely allied system to Nyaya is the Vaisheshika system, founded by Kanada Kashyapa. The name derives from the fact that the school dwells upon *vishesha* as a category of knowledge.

The most important systematic work on this school is the *Vaisheshika Sutra* written by Kanada. It was followed by many other commentaries.

While they are agreed on many aspects of philosophy, there are important differences between Nyaya and Vaisheshika. *Nyaya* accepts four independent sources of knowledge - perception, inference, comparison and testimony. The Vaisheshika system admits to only two sources - perception and inference. But the Vaisheshika system accepts the Vedas as a valid source of testimony.

The Nyaya system enumerates sixteen *padarthas*, which form the basic premise of the system. On the other hand, Vaisheshika recognizes seven *padarthas* (see Box).

Seven *Padarthas* (Categories) Recognized by Vaisheshika

1. *Dravya* (substance)
2. *Guna* (quality)
3. *Karma* (action)
4. *Samanya* (generality)
5. *Vishesha* (particularity)
6. *Samavaya* (relation of inherence)
7. *Abhava* (non-existence)

Dravya has nine components, viz., *prithvi* (earth), *ap* (water), *tejas* (fire), *vayu* (air), *akasa* (ether), *kala* (time), *dik* (space), *atman* (self or soul) and *manas* (mind). The first five are called *panchabhuta*s since they have specific qualities that can be perceived by one or the other of our external senses.

A *guna* (quality) exists in a substance and has no independent existence or activity. *Rupa* (colour), *rasa* (taste) and *sparsha* (touch) are some of the *guna*s that we come across in substances.

Similarly, other categories have specific interpretations.

Atomic Naturalism

*Darshana*s have different concepts of nature. The idea of naturalism tries to align philosophy with science and the natural world, without falling into the realm of the supernatural.

There are many types of naturalism. Ontological naturalism argues that reality is devoid of supernatural entities. Methodological naturalism advises that philosophical enquiry should be conducted using scientific methods. Moral naturalism expounds that moral facts are a part of the natural world.

In the world of Vaisheshika, there are two parts – the eternal, unchanging part and the non-eternal, ever-changing part. The atomic theory of Vaisheshika is of special importance and explains the non-eternal part of the world, which is periodically created and destroyed.

The eternal part of the world comprises, apart from the supreme being who created it, the four kinds of atoms of earth, water, fire and air. These can neither be created nor destroyed. Along with them, the five substances – ether, space, time, mind and soul – are also eternal constituents of the universe.

On the other hand, all objects containing more than one atom can be created and destroyed. The simplest combination is that of two atoms of the same type, called the *dvyanuka*. A combination of three *dvyanukas* is called *tryanuka*. Other larger compounds contain more than three atoms. The atom (*parmanu*) and the *dvyanuka* cannot be perceived and can be known only through inference. The smallest particle that can be perceived is the *tryanuka*. In all this, each atom has its own attribute due to the principle of *vishesha*, the differentiator.

> **Vaisheshika Sutra**
>
> The sutra was composed by Kanada Kashyapa and mentions the Saankhya and Mimansa schools. But it leaves out Buddhism and Jainism, which made scholars conclude that it is dated earlier than these two schools. Generally, the date of the sutra is believed to be between the sixth century BCE and the second century BCE.
>
> There are several commentaries on the sutra. The most prominent are the Padartha Dharma Sangraha of Prashastapada and Mathichandra's Dasha Padartha Sastra. This was translated into Chinese in 648 CE by Yuanzhuang.
>
> This sutra is one of the earliest systematic documents on ontology (the study of being, existence and reality). A sophisticated theory is presented on the creation and existence of the universe using naturalistic atomism. Its analysis of motion as the cause of all phenomena in the world is regarded as one of the earliest texts on physics in human history.

It is possible that triads of different elements combine to form tetrads, and so on. Since the atoms of different elements have different qualities, the triads have different structural arrangements. Therefore, large composite substances that are made up of a combination of triads and larger entities will exhibit different qualities.

All the objects in the world are made by atoms joining together into a compound. What drives them to activity? What are the conditions for their combination? The objects in the universe and living beings are a combination of atoms. But living beings have souls, which are eternal and carry the karma of the individual from one birth to another. So, the whole world is a moral order where atoms combine according to the will of god (Ishwara), who creates and destroys the world guided by a particular purpose. God creates the universe so that individuals can experience pleasure and pain according to their previously earned merit. When the time comes, god destroys the world to relieve individuals of the suffering they have gone through over many lives. One complete cycle of creation and destruction is called kalpa.

Differences between Vaisheshika and Nyaya Systems		
Founder	Kanada	Gautama
Period	600 BCE	500 BCE
Origin of name	*Vishesha* (particular)	*Nyaya* (logic)
Categories	7	16
Valid source of knowledge	Perception, inference	Perception, inference, comparison and testimony
Approach	Naturalist atomism	Non-atomist
Emphasis	Metaphysics	Epistemology

Key Takeaways

- The Nyaya system of philosophy gives primary importance to the acquiring of true knowledge of reality and the conditions required to achieve that.
- The school was founded by Gautama Aksapada, the author of the *Nyaya Sutras*.
- Nyaya is also known by other names, such as Tarkashastra (the science of reasoning) and Anvikshiki (the science of critical inquiry).
- The Naiyayikas (Nyaya scholars) accepted four means of obtaining valid knowledge (*pramana*) – perception (*pratyaksha*), inference (*anumana*), comparison (*upamana*) and the testimony of reliable sources (*shabda*).
- Sixteen philosophical topics (*padartha*) make up the Nyaya system.
- In the Nayaya concept of vada, the person putting forward a view (*vadi*) and the person refuting it (*prativadi*) debate with each other using valid methods and hypothetical arguments to arrive at the truth.
- Nyaya believes in the existence of the eternal soul and god and the theory of karma.
- The earliest formal document on the method of conducting debates is the *Charaka Samhita* (see chapter on Ayurveda philosophy). The *Nyaya Sutra* further systematized the theory of debating.

Fact Check (Answers at the Back)

1. What is the primary aim of the Nyaya system of philosophy?
   a. To teach the art of sculpture and painting to its students.
   b. To advocate for the importance of physical strength and exercise.
   c. To inculcate the powers of logical reasoning and a rigorous critical approach in its students.
   d. To focus exclusively on the study of ancient texts without interpretation or criticism.

2. The Nyaya system accepts four means of valid knowledge. (Yes, No)
3. Pramana represents a valid means of obtaining true knowledge. (Yes, No)
4. What is Nyaya's critique of the doctrine of momentariness as proposed by Buddhism?
   a. Nyaya agrees with the doctrine, stating that everything in the external world is indeed momentary and lacks permanence.
   b. Nyaya argues that the doctrine goes against our normal experiences because there needs to be continuity for the cycle of cause and effect to persist.
   c. Nyaya supports the doctrine but argues that it does not apply to consciousness and the soul.
   d. Nyaya believes the doctrine is fully accurate but poorly explained by Buddhist scholars.
5. Samshaya represents the state of uncertainty, wavering and doubt. (Yes, No)
6. Nyaya does not believe in the existence of the soul. (Yes, No)
7. Nyaya declares that god is the efficient cause of the universe. (Yes, No)

11

Mimansa: Putting Rituals above God

A school of philosophy that is closely related to the Vedanta school, as we shall see in this chapter, is the Mimansa school. The word 'mimansa' means 'finding a solution through critical investigation'. The tradition is also called Poorva-Mimansa because it focuses on the earlier Vedic texts, which are more preoccupied with ritual actions and their benefits. The Mimansa texts not only lay down clear-cut rules for conducting rituals but also provide philosophical justification for the beliefs on which they are based. The philosophical aspect of Mimansa is what we are interested in here.

Timeline of **Mimansa**

5th–4th century BCE	*Poorva Mīmaṃsa Sutras* of Jaimini
5th–6th century CE	Commentary by Sabaraswami
7th–8th century CE	Commentaries by Kumarila Bhaṭṭa and Prabhakara

To justify rituals, the Mimansa doctrine attempts to establish the existence of the soul, which can carry forward the fruits of conducting rituals even after the body dies. So, one is assured that there is some power that preserves the fruits of rituals performed in this world and makes sure that they are tagged to the soul for enjoying future rewards. The doctrine also tries to establish the infallibility of the Vedas and the fact that this world is real and actions performed here during one's life matter.

In this, it is opposed to schools such as Buddhism and Jainism, which deny the existence of souls and the reality of this world. Other schools oppose the idea that rituals are an end in themselves.

The foundation of this school was laid in Jaimini's Poorva Mīmaṃsa Sutras. A major commentary on the sutra was written by Sabaraswami. Though there are several commentators, the two most important are Prabhakara and Kumarila Bhaṭṭa, who founded the two different schools of Mimansa.

How Do We Acquire Knowledge?

As with other schools, the Mimansa school also delves deeply into the nature and valid sources of knowledge. Later, the Vedanta school extensively drew upon this work.

The Validity of Knowledge

Mimansa argues that knowledge is self-evident. This is based on experience. In our daily lives, when we see an object, we believe in its validity; we don't wait to test its validity by inference or argument. When we see a blue jug, we don't test the validity of our observation. We acknowledge it as a blue jug. We believe in knowledge as soon as it arises. If our observation is not contradicted by others, then we believe in the knowledge all the more. Of course, if our eyes had been defective or we had observed in the dark, then knowledge would not have arisen in the first place.

Therefore, Mimansa believes that i) the very conditions from which knowledge arises also confirm its validity, and ii) this knowledge needs no verification by another source such as inference. This is the theory of intrinsic validity (*svatah-pramanya-vada*). According to this theory, truth is self-evident. If, at a later stage, our observation is disproved, then the knowledge we have gained is false.

The Nyaya school disagrees with this theory. The school believes that all knowledge needs to be validated by some external conditions, such as inference. When we perceive a blue jug through our eyes, how can we believe that our sense organs will not deceive us? Moreover, acquiring knowledge is a mental act. It cannot be guaranteed that a blue jug means the same to everyone. It can be validated only by others' inferences. Also, all knowledge is produced by a coming together of several causes, and therefore, is dependent on external factors. If, as the Mimansa school says, the production of knowledge also self-validates it, then there would be no illusion. Even a mirage will become objectively true. Therefore, the validity of knowledge can be ascertained only by experiencing the object pertaining to that knowledge. If a mirage does not lead to water, then the knowledge becomes invalid. This is the theory of extrinsic validity (*paratah-pramanya-vada*).

The Mimansa school argues that if this were to be accepted, then an infinite regress would happen because even that inference would need another inference to validate it, and this process would continue ad infinitum. When we see a tiger, we run away and don't wait for knowledge to be validated by another source.

The position of Mimansa can be understood from the fact that the school had to prove that the Veda is self-valid and did not require God to confirm its validity. The Vedic rituals have to be followed without requiring any test. By the same token, Mimansa is opposed to pralaya, the doctrine of creation and destruction, which, if acknowledged, would mean that the Vedas are not eternal.

According to Mimansa, we can gain knowledge only from something that exists. When we look at an object, recognition comes in two steps. In the first step, we gain a mere awareness of the object. This is indeterminate perception. We think, it may be a rope or a snake. In the next stage, we get more details about the object, such as its quality, name, etc. This is determinate perception. We conclude, this is a rope. Even though there are two stages of recognition, the mind implicitly forms an opinion about the object in the first stage itself, which is confirmed later based on past experiences. For example, a person cannot perceive a cow in the first stage and then come to a judgement that, after all, it is a man in the second stage. Though the mind takes a little bit of time to arrive at a correct judgement of an object, the object is itself real, not illusory, contrary to what Buddhists and Vedantists think.

In addition to perception, the Prabhakara school accepts four other valid sources of knowledge: i) inference (*anumana*), ii) comparison (*upamana*), iii) testimony from authoritative sources (*shabda*) and iv) postulation (*arthapatti*). The Bhaṭṭa school adds a fifth valid source, non-perception (*anupalabdi*).

We have already come across perception and inference in other schools of philosophy.

We have also seen that the Nyaya school admits comparison as a valid source. However, there is a difference in its application in the Mimansa school. According to Mimansa, one derives knowledge through comparison when one perceives a present object and concludes its nature from an object perceived in the past. For example, when one sees a rat for the first time, one can conclude that it resembles a mouse that the person has seen in the past. This method is strictly not perception since only one of the objects is being perceived. The other similar object it is being compared to is just a memory.

Mimansa gives special importance to shabda as a source of knowledge since its philosophical premise is entirely dependent on the authority of the Vedas. Even with respect to authority, Mimansa is concerned only about the impersonal authority of the Vedas and not the personal authority of individual sages. All its arguments connected to the soul, rebirth and the reality of this world are connected to the performance of this or that ritual. That is the reason for it being called the philosophy of Ritualistic Pragmatism–it believes all knowledge should serve or arise from a ritualistic activity.

The Mimansa school considers Vedic authority as impersonal, and hence, dismisses the need for a personal god. The Vedas are eternal and have no single creator. The hymns were revealed and are not the creation of any seers, though Vedic texts contain the names of several sages. Just because they have been composed in a human language doesn't mean that they are non-eternal. The fruits of rituals could not have been observed by anyone. Therefore, the Vedas are not the product of some authors.

The next source of knowledge, postulation (*arthapatti*), gains importance when a certain phenomenon can be explained only by the supposition of an unperceived fact. If, for example, a phenomenon such as a man putting on weight even when he had been fasting requires one to postulate a reason. The postulate can be that he eats in the night while others are sleeping. This kind of knowledge differs from perception, inference and words of authority. We come across this method many times in our day-to-day activities. For example, if a sentence is incomplete, such as 'shut it', we postulate that it must be related to shutting a door or a window.

Non-perception (*anupalabdi*) can also be a source of knowledge according to Bhaṭṭa Mimansa and Advaita Vedanta. How can we confirm the non-existence of an object? For example, if someone says, 'The jar is not on the table,' how can it be confirmed? An obvious answer is that since it is not perceived by our senses, we can confidently say that the jar is not on the table. This kind of knowledge does not fall within the realm of other means of acquiring knowledge, such as inference, testimony or comparison. Therefore, non-perception is an additional means of valid knowledge. Of course, if we cannot see the jar in the night or the atoms making up the jar, or we cannot see a quality such as happiness, we do not conclude that they are non-existent. The method of non-perception applies only to certain circumstances.

Normally, in our day-to-day activities, we act on knowledge from perception, inference or testimony if there are reasonable conditions present. For example, we would believe immediately that a jar is on the table if there is sufficient light and our eyes are not defective. Similarly, when we hear words that are meaningful and appropriate to the situation, then we do not doubt their validity. Therefore, the Mimansa concludes that: i) the very conditions under which knowledge is acquired ensure the validity of the knowledge itself, and ii) as soon as a person acquires the knowledge, its validity is confirmed, and there is no requirement for verification. Thus, Mimansa believes that there is intrinsic validity in knowledge gained through sources as explained above.

The Nature of Reality

Buddhists do not believe that the world and its objects are real. They believe in theories of voidness and momentariness as we saw earlier. The Advaita Vedantists claim that the world is just an illusion. The Mimansa school, on the other hand, believes in the reality of the world and its objects. Some objects can be perceived directly. Others can be understood through other sources of knowledge, such as inference. In this way, Mimansa claims to be more materialistic in its outlook than many other schools of philosophy. According to the Mimansa doctrine, souls, as well as other material elements of reality, are permanent substances. The world consists of living beings and non-living substances. Living bodies live by the law of karma, they reap the consequences of their past deeds and continue their suffering and enjoyment in this world. The sensory organs are instruments that enable them to go through this suffering and enjoyment. The objects of the world constitute that which can be enjoyed or suffered. So, the Mimansa philosophy does not admit the existence of a god. Unlike Vaisheshika, Mimansa does not require a god to arrange the atoms in a particular way. It is the law of karma that regulates the arrangement and combination of atoms. Since all the objects are eternal, the world is neither created nor destroyed by a supreme being. Notwithstanding these major differences with Vaisheshika, the Mimasakas follow their conception of *padarthas* and the sub-categories within them.

Thus, the focus of the Mimansa school was on epistemology and metaphysics of the concept of dharma, which meant rituals and social duties. It was not concerned about the existence of a supreme being. For the Mimasakas, the Vedas hold all the truth; they are infallible, and rituals are the ultimate pathway to liberation.

Theism and Atheism in Indian Thought

The popular perception that Indian systems of philosophy (*darshanas*) are mainly concerned with the existence of god and the periodic creation and destruction of the universe is an unfortunate misconception.

The atheistic schools, such as the Charvakas, Buddhism and Jainism, do propagate the non-requirement of a god in the functioning of the universe. But even among other 'conformative' schools, such as Saankhya and Mimansa, there are atheistic conceptions. Therefore, the division of *darshanas* into *astika* and *nastika* is not based on their conception of the existence or non-existence of a god but on whether they accept the Vedas as the ultimate, infallible authority or not.

Ishwarakrishna's Saankhya Karika rejects the possibility of an all-powerful creator of the universe. Other Saankhya texts, too, endorse this stand. We just saw that Poorva Mīmaṃsa Sutras endorses the authority of the Vedas and its rituals but emphatically denies the need for a supreme being to run the affairs of the world. Even in Patanjali's Yoga Sutra, the presence of a god is side-lined. Nyaya texts, too, are far less convincing about the need for a god.

Shankara's Advaita Vedanta, while emphasizing on acquiring knowledge, does advocate the existence of a Brahman. But Advaita Vedanta is one of the many darshanas and does not claim to represent all Indian thought. However, it acquired importance in the nineteenth century thanks to native intellectuals who wanted to counteract the 'material West' with the idea of a 'spiritual India'.

Nevertheless, the atheism of Indian schools cannot be equated to the modern conception of materialism. Many of the schools accept the existence of a permanent soul and the theory of karma, the cycle of birth and death and so on .

Jaimini's Sutra

The author of the Mimansa Sutras is Jaimini. Later Sabaraswami wrote a commentary on the sutras. Kumarila Bhaṭṭa and his pupil, Prabhakara, took the elaboration of the Mimansa school of philosophy further, as we have noted earlier.

> **Rituals vs Knowledge**
>
> Jaimini's guru was Badarayana, the author of the Brahma Sutras and founder of the Vedanta school.
>
> The guru and shishya (student) respected each other and quoted each other in their works but differed violently in their philosophical outlook.
>
> For Badarayana, knowledge was the ultimate path to liberation.
>
> Jaimini emphasized on rituals to attain moksha.
>
> They were thus the antithesis of the other.

Not much is known about how the sacrificial system of worship first put forward in the Brahmanas grew in Indian thought and spawned a network of rituals. With the popularity of rituals growing, at one point in time, the necessity for collecting the rules and regulations into a written treatise became important. The rituals were getting increasingly complex. This could have spurred the rationalization of various rituals into Mimansa literature. In this, Jaimini's Mimansa Sutras were not the only compilation of merit, since he himself mentions several earlier exponents, but it is also the only sutra to have survived. Not all of it may have been Jaimini's original contribution.

The most popular commentary on the sutras is the Sabara Bhashya. Kumarila Bhaṭṭa, who was probably a senior contemporary of Shankaracharya (788 CE), wrote the well-known exposition of Sabara Bhashya. Kumarila is referred to by his followers as just Bhaṭṭa. There were many other commentators, but Kumarila's pupil Prabhakara, often called *gurumata* because his teacher himself praised him as his guru, is the most known.

Mimansa literature has great value for a practising Hindu since it is the most authoritative text on Vedic rituals even today.

After Kumarila and Prabhakara, Mimansa literature did not see any significant additions. The Mimansa Sutras are mostly concerned with Vedic texts related to sacrifices and rituals. There is not much philosophy in them .

The Two Mimansas

The Mimansa doctrine described in this chapter is called Poorva Mimansa. Before we proceed to the next chapter on Vedanta, which is called Uttara Mimansa, let us look at the difference between the two Mimansas.

All Vedic texts, including the Samhitas and Brahmanas, need some explanatory texts and commentaries, such as Sayana's commentaries on the Samhitas and Brahmanas, and the *bhashyas* credited to Shankara on the principal Upanishads. Without these explanatory texts, a student of Vedic literature will be at a loss to understand the context and inter-relationship of the sutras contained in these texts. But the commentaries themselves are also an explanation of each sutra and not the inner essence of the whole of which they form a part.

> **Jaimini**
>
> Sage Jaimini was the founder of the Mimansa school, one of the i. He is believed to be the disciple of Sage Veda Vyasa. He was the author of the Mimansa Sutras and Jaimini Sutras. He lived around the fourth to the second century BCE.

The task of systematizing Vedic writings, smoothening out the apparent contradictions and connecting the meaning of various sacred texts into a separate sastra or doctrine is called Mimansa.

The Poorva Mimansa systematizes *karmakanda*, i.e., the portion of Vedic texts concerned with rituals and sacrifices. These are drawn from the Samhitas and the Brahmanas, leaving out the Aranyaka portions. Its subject is the practice of rituals.

The Uttara Mimansa systematizes jnanakanda, which relates to the Vedic sacred texts comprising the Aranyaka portions of the Brahmanas and the various Upanishads. It's subject is the knowledge of the ultimate reality, the Brahman.

The requirement for Poorva Mimansa must have come up very early since there were doubts and debates on the correct performance of rituals among its practitioners. A guidebook on how to perform rituals in conformity with Vedic teachings was in demand. An authoritative compilation of the rituals and sacrifices was also the need of the time for Vedic philosophical schools to counter the attack of Buddhism, Jainism and other non-conformative schools. This task was relatively easier since it involved a study of a limited extent of texts and could be accomplished in a reasonably short time. A certain amount of flexibility was provided so that followers of different Vedic schools could perform a sacrifice in different ways.

Uttara Mimansa, on the other hand, was not as urgently required as Poorva Mimansa. So work on it started later and involved recent additions to the Vedic corpus, the Upanishads. The exercise of attaining knowledge was not connected with performing rituals. The scholars who were engaged in this exercise realized that while rules concerning rituals may be flexible, those concerning the nature of the Brahman, the relationship between the body and soul and between the individual and universal selves had to be accurate and consistent with the whole body of the Upanishads. This was a much more challenging and cumbersome task. As compared to *karmakanda, jnanakanda* required a systematic defence. *Karmakanda* was practised only by the higher castes while *jnanakanda* was theoretically accessible to all, including women. There is evidence of Kshatriyas and women of higher castes participating in philosophical debates.

So, today, there is a vast body of literature belonging to the two distinct branches of the Mimansa school. We have, on the one hand, the Mimansa Sastra and on the other, the Vedanta Sastra.

The two most important works of these two branches of Mimansa are the sutras of Jaimini and Badarayana. The writing of these sutras must have involved a thorough analysis of earlier texts, of which there are many references. These sutras not only summarized earlier works, but they also provided impetus for philosophical enquiry up to the present day.

Key Takeaways

- Poorva Mimansa, or Mimansa, is closely related to the Vedanta school.
- Mimansa not only lays down clear-cut rules for conducting rituals but also provides philosophical justification for the beliefs on which they are based.
- It believes in the existence of the soul, the infallibility of the Vedas and the fact that this world is real and actions performed here during one's life matter.
- In addition to perception, the Prabhakara school accepts four other valid sources of knowledge: i) inference (*anumana*), ii) comparison (*upamana*), iii) testimony from authoritative sources (*shabda*) and iv) postulation (*arthapatti*). The Bhaṭṭa school adds a fifth valid source, non-perception (*anupalabdi*).
- Mimansa gives special importance to shabda as a source of knowledge since its philosophical premise is entirely dependent on the authority of the Vedas.
- The Mimansa philosophy does not admit the existence of a god.
- For the Mimasakas, the Vedas hold all the truth; they are infallible, and rituals are the ultimate pathway to liberation.

Fact Check (Answers at the Back)

1. According to the Mimansa doctrine, souls, as well as other material elements of reality, are illusions. (Yes, No)
2. Mimansa considers the performance of rituals and sacrifices as the ultimate pathway to moksha. (Yes, No)
3. The division of darshanas into astika and nastika is not based on their conception of the existence or non-existence of a god but on whether they accept the Vedas as the ultimate, infallible authority. (Yes, No)
4. The author of the Mimansa Sutras is Kapila. (Yes, No)
5. Vedic texts are difficult to understand without commentaries. (Yes, No)

6. Which of the following best describes the primary focus of Poorva Mimansa and Uttara Mimansa, respectively?
    a. Poorva Mimansa is concerned with rituals and sacrifices, while Uttara Mimansa focuses on the knowledge of ultimate reality.
    b. Poorva Mimansa emphasizes attaining knowledge, whereas Uttara Mimansa centres on performing rituals.
    c. Poorva Mimansa explores the relationship between the body and soul, while Uttara Mimansa delves into Vedic teachings on sacrifices.
    d. Poorva Mimansa deals with philosophical debates involving women, while Uttara Mimansa is limited to higher castes.
7. Why did the need for Poorva Mimansa arise earlier than that of Uttara Mimansa?
    a. Poorva Mimansa was needed to counter the influence of non-conformative schools, while Uttara Mimansa was not required for defence purposes.
    b. Poorva Mimansa had to address doubts and debates on correct ritual performance, whereas Uttara Mimansa was focused on recent additions to the Vedic corpus.
    c. Poorva Mimansa was associated with flexibility in performing sacrifices, whereas Uttara Mimansa required an accurate understanding of the nature of Brahman.
    d. Poorva Mimansa involved the study of a limited extent of texts and demanded a guidebook for rituals, making it a relatively easier task compared to Uttara Mimansa.

12

Vedanta: The All-Powerful Brahman

We have seen so far that arriving at the truth has been the paramount objective of all Indian schools of philosophy. All of them have explained the sources of valid knowledge, *pramana*, in detail. They have discussed the validity of knowledge thus obtained, *pramanya*. The *pramanya* has not only an epistemological significance (how do we acquire knowledge and the validity of the knowledge) but also a metaphysical one (the origin of the universe, the question of the soul, etc.).

Many of the philosophical works would first employ dialectical reasoning to criticize and expose the inconsistencies of the competing schools of thought before elaborating on the theoretical underpinnings of their own school.

> "We hear of extensive tours undertaken by the Buddha, Mahavira and Shankara to propagate their views and win over followers. So, often these debates were not conducted merely with the objective of seeking truth. Often, they were contests to elevate one's own school of philosophy and put down the opponent's."

As we have seen, Indian schools of philosophy accept one or more of the six *pramanas* as the correct means of accurate knowledge and truths:

They are i) *pratyaksa* (perception), ii) *anumana* (inference), iii) *upamana* (comparison and analogy), iv) *arthapatti* (postulation, derivation), v) *anupalabdi* (non-perception, negative/cognitive proof) and vi) *shabda* (word, testimony of past or present reliable experts).

Below is a comparative table of valid means of accurate knowledge across these schools.

Philosophy School	Valid Means of Accurate Knowledge
Charvaka school	The Charvaka school accepted only perception as a valid source of knowledge. All remaining methods are invalid or prone to error, and therefore, invalid.
Vaisheshika school	The Vaisheṣhika school considered the following as the only proper means of knowledge: • Perception (*pratyaksa*) • Inference (*anumana*)
Saankhya, Yoga, Vishishtadvaita Vedanta and Dvaita Vedanta schools	Proper means of knowledge must rely on these three pramanas: • Perception (*pratyaksa*) • Inference (*anumana*) • Testimony/word of reliable experts (*shabda*)
Nyaya school	The Nyaya school accepts four means of obtaining knowledge (*pramana*): • Perception (*pratyaksa*) • Inference (*anumana*) • Comparison (*upamana*) • Word (*shabda*)
Prabhakara Mimansa school	These are valid sources of knowledge: • Perception (*pratyaksa*) • Inference (*anumana*) • Word, testimony (*shabda*) • Comparison, analogy (*upamana*) • Postulation, presumption (*arthapatti*)

Advaita Vedanta and Bhaṭṭa Mimansa schools	The following pramanas are accepted in this school: • Perception (*pratyaksa*) • Inference (*anumana*) • Word, testimony (*shabda*) • Comparison, analogy (*upamana*) • Postulation, presumption (*arthapatti*) • Non-perception, cognitive proof using non-existence (*anupalabdi*, *abhava*)
Buddhism	These are valid pramanas: • Perception (*pratyaksa*) • Inference (*anumana*)

Figure 15: *Valid sources of knowledge across schools of philosophy*

The Literature of the Vedanta

Vedanta philosophy concerns itself with the elaboration of the philosophy contained in the Upanishads, which has been summarized in the Brahma Sutras authored by Badarayana. Since the Upanishads form the tail-end of the literature connected with the Vedas, its philosophy is called the Uttara-Mimansa. The philosophy of the earlier part of the Veda literature is called just Mimansa, which was the focus of the previous chapter.

Several learned scholars have written commentaries on the Brahma Sutras, but the one written by Shankaracharya, also among the earliest, is the most popular. So colossal has been the contribution of Shankara to Vedanta philosophy that today Vedanta philosophy is indistinguishable from Shankara's philosophy. Other trends of Vedanta philosophy expounded by scholars such as Madhavacharya, Ramanuja and Vallabha specifically bear the author's name and are considered as variants of Shankara's philosophy, though they are widely divergent.

> **The Upanishads**
>
> The Upanishads were the tail end of Vedic literature. Vedic literature can be classified into three kinds.
>
> The first category contains the Vedic hymns and mantras compiled into the Samhitas made up the Rig, Yajur, Sama and Atharva Vedas. The second category consists of the Brahmanas (no relation to Brahmins), which are basically instructional material for conducting rituals.
>
> The third part is the Upanishads, which delve into philosophical issues.
>
> All three categories of texts are considered revealed texts (*srutis*), and divine commandments.
>
> In a way, the three categories also relate to the three stages of a man's life, the Vedas coming first, the Brahmanas for the householder doing his ritual duties and the Upanishads for the older individual when he retires to the forest.

The Advaita Philosophy of Shankara

Many schools of thought we have seen have sutras, which provide the philosophical foundation for the school. In the case of the Vedanta system, the sutras and Upanishads served as the foundational material. The sutras are extremely condensed aphorisms that needed interpretation by commentators. The Upanishads were many, and Badarayana's Brahma Sutras systematized their viewpoints and tried to present the harmony inherent in them.

The Upanishads are sacred commandments like the Vedas and Brahmanas. Shankara, who was born in the eighth century CE in the Malabar area of present-day Kerala, was not the sole founder

> **The Brahma Sutras**
>
> Upanishad means sitting near the teacher in order to overcome ignorance. The Upanishads were taught only by a guru at his *gurukul* to select pupils. The teachings were not open to all.
>
> There were many Upanishads, at least 112, developed at different points in time by different seers. There were points of unity and difference. There was a need to systematize the writings and present a cogent view of the philosophy residing in the various texts. Badarayana's Brahma Sutras accomplished this. It outlines in four chapters: i) the coherence latent in the Upanishads, ii) their harmony with respect to theories of knowledge and rules of logic, iii) the means to realize truth and iv) the benefit of realizing the ultimate truth.
>
> Badarayana's sutras were terse and required interpretation. Many scholars came forward to do this. Each one claimed that their interpretation was the most truthful, though they were all unanimous in the belief that the sutras truly presented the Upanishads in a nutshell. The authors of these commentaries became the founders of the particular school of Vedanta. Thus we have the Vedanta schools of Shankara, Madhava, Ramanuja, Vallabha and so on. Today, these schools of Vedanta philosophy have touched the lives of billions of people.

of any system since the Vedanta system had many exponents. He took up the task of commenting on the Brahma Sutras and the Upanishads to establish his interpretation of them as the perfect one. If that could be done, then his philosophy based on the highest authority would have no opponents.

In this endeavour, the Mimansists gave a lot of trouble since they held the view that the Vedas were, in the final analysis, guides for conducting rituals, not philosophical texts. Shankara did not contest the argument that the Vedas were commandments. But he argued that the Upanishads were not mandatory injunctions. They were required to be interpreted to prove that the only path to salvation is to attain knowledge of the Absolute, the Brahman. He explained that the mandatory rituals described in the Vedas and Brahmanas were for the ordinary people who craved material benefits, while the Upanishads were meant for the wise who detested material benefits and earthly pleasures.

Shankara did not take the route that founders of other philosophical schools took to develop various components of philosophical enquiry logically. He compared texts of the various Upanishads and tried to establish that there was harmony among them in unravelling the nature of Brahman as the way to know the ultimate truth. During this effort, he systematized various thoughts in the Upanishads and criticized opponents of the theory of Brahman, exposing their inconsistencies wherever he could. He had to particularly argue vehemently against the doctrines of *mahat* and *prakriti* of the early Saankhya school and the realistic categories of the Nyaya school[1].

> **The Shankara bhashya considers the Brahman, the highest self, as different, as well as superior, to a particular deity such as Shiva or Vishnu, who had been the most popular gods of worship for centuries before Shankara.**

Shankara's popularity as the most authoritative commentator on the sutras relating to the Upanishads hides the fact that his interpretation does not stand up to strict scrutiny in that it does not apply the well-tested rules of philosophical enquiry but just asserts that Brahman is the absolute truth and that this conclusion is based on the sacred authority of Vedic texts. In modern times, Shankara's interpretation is held above doubt or dispute. However, a modern investigator engaged in philosophical enquiry has to subject all interpretations of the Vedic texts to critical assessments.

At any rate, the Vedanta Sutras (also called Brahma Sutras) have come to acquire an uncontested authority over the centuries. Many commentaries have been made before Shankara and many after. It is not possible to delve deeply into these commentaries for want of space and time. In the following sections, we will discuss a few important contributions to Vedanta.

The Life of Shankara

Shankara was born in the eighth century in the Malabar area of present-day Kerala in a Brahmin family. There are many myths about him, and he is often described as the incarnation of Shiva himself. He is believed to have turned an ascetic as early as his eighth year and written his famed commentary on the Brahma Sutras in his twelfth year. Commentaries on tẹn Upanishads are attributed to him. Keeping Benares as the base, he ventured to all parts of India, engaging followers of other schools of thought in debates and often defeating them. He even challenged Kumarila Bhaṭṭa, who was on the verge of his death, and hence, had to take on his disciple.

His variant of Vedanta preached *advaita*, non-dualism. In his commentary on the Brahma Sutras, he took great pains to criticise the advocates of Advaita Vedanta, on the lines of the Saankhya philosophy.

The Brahman

The essence of Shankara's Vedanta philosophy is that Brahman is the only thing existing in the world; it is pure intelligence, being and blessedness. Though we think there are many individual selves, there is only one self called the Brahman. Our illusion about the world of objects comes from the fact that we identify our individual selves with these illusory objects, and consequently, they appear real to us.

> The world of illusion can be explained by using the analogy of clay and objects made out of clay. Though clay may be moulded into plates, jugs and cups, they are appearances of clay with different names and forms. The final reality is clay. Similarly, this world of objects is just an appearance of the Brahman in different names and forms. The final reality is Brahman.

If one accepts the existence of the individual self and the world of objects, then one has to explain their presence by conceiving a god (Ishwara) who created the world. But once the person realizes that the world is illusory and that there is only one self of which all are a part, then there would be no need for a creator. The creator also becomes illusory. In the final analysis, it is Brahman that is both the material cause as well the efficient cause of the world. In fact, the effect is itself an illusory appendage of the cause since there is no individual self and no world of objects.

The main idea presented by Shankara's Advaita Vedanta school is that the ultimate and absolute truth is the self. It may appear as different selves, and these different selves may experience a world of many objects, but these are illusory. Other systems of philosophy identified *pramanas*, by which they could be sure of acquiring valid knowledge in practical life. But the Vedanta of Shankara is not interested in this illusory world. It is interested only in the ultimate truth governing the microcosm and the macrocosm. That ultimate truth is the Brahman. When one's mind is purged of all passions and desires, then the soul is ready to comprehend the highest truth, 'That art thou.' Then the individual becomes truth himself. There is no notion of 'mine' and 'yours'.

In this, Advaita Vedanta differs from other systems of philosophy. Other systems propagated that when man is rid of all passions and desires, his soul is detached from bodily desires, when he is rid of all consciousness of himself, then he is ready to venture on the path of moksha, salvation. But even after he is rid of worldly desires, the world continues to operate, since the world is not an illusion. The world was a reality. The problem was that the individual self identified itself with the body, mind and ego and started indulging in the world of joy and sorrow. His experiences in the world were guided by his accumulated karma and the cycle of false relationships of the soul with the world continued.

Only when the soul dissociated itself from worldly desires and returned to its pure state, could one liberate themselves from the endless cycle. The Nyaya, Vaisheshika and Mimansa schools regarded this pure state of self as an unconscious state. The Saankhya and Yoga systems regarded this state as a state of pure intelligence .

The Philosophy of Gaudapada

Shankara's teachings on the Advaita Vedanta philosophy say that the ultimate and absolute truth is the self. The individual selves and the world of objects are just illusions. There is actually only one self, and that is Brahman.

Whether the Advaita philosophy is being practised in the real sense or not, the philosophy itself has gained wide acceptance among Indians. It is important to understand the beginnings of Advaita from where Shankara developed it further. It is also gainful to understand revisions and re-interpretation of Advaita philosophy by later exponents. In this respect, we will be discussing here the ideas put forward by Gaudapada, who lived before Shankara, and the ideas of Ramanuja and Madhava, who came after Shankara.

Gaudapada was called Paramaguru by Shankara. He is believed to be the teacher of Govinda, who was, in turn, the teacher of Shankara. He is the author of the *Mandukya Karika*, which was a commentary on the Mandukya Upanishad, though some say that the *Karika* is the work of several authors composed at different times. His work shows that he was influenced by Buddhism even though his main contribution was towards Advaita Vedanta philosophy.

Gaudapada is estimated to have lived around the sixth or seventh century. Since he was Shankara's teacher's teacher, there must have been a gap of many decades between Shankara and Gaudapada. Several Buddhist scholars who lived in the sixth century have quoted Gaudapada's works. Gaudapada himself quotes Buddhist scholars Nagarjuna and Asanga, who lived in the fourth to fifth centuries.

Though the *Mandukya Karika* is not the oldest work on Advaita Vedanta, its systematic presentation has made it a reliable source for later Vedanta scholars. It is divided into four chapters. The first chapter interprets the Mandukya Upanishad. Gaudapada describes four states of the existence of the self: awake, dream-filled sleep, deep sleep, and beyond deep sleep. In the second chapter, he explains that what we experience in the dream state and the awake state about the external world is unreal. Just as mistaking a rope for a snake in the dark, our mind constructs realities that don't exist.

In the third chapter, Gaudapada explains that nothing comes into being and nothing goes out of extinction. There is only Brahman, which has neither a beginning nor an end. Confusing individual souls with the universal soul is like confusing the space around us with the spaces enclosed in jars. When the jars are broken, the individual spaces within the jars merge with the vast space around us. In the same way, when the individual self breaks out of illusion, it merges with the universal self.

Basing himself on the Upanishads, such as the Brihadaranyaka Upanishad, he argues that that one's own *atman* (self) is identical to the *atman* in other beings, and all *atman* are identical with the Brahman.

The fourth chapter, called 'Atlashanti' (extinction of coal) uses the dialectical method of argument to explain the path to realizing the ultimate truth. All appearances are without death or decay. The argument that a cause contains with it the effect does not hold water because the cause is not unchanging; it is itself the effect of another cause. It is not possible that things come into being from that which has no production. In the same way, it is not possible to accept that something that was itself produced can become the cause of an effect. If we accept this, then it will mean we accept endless regression (*anavastha*). Since nothing is produced, there is no cause and effect. The mind only projects objects and makes them appear real. It does not itself come into touch with these objects. Therefore, neither the mind nor the objects seen by it are produced. Though there is an appearance of production of objects, the one reality is Brahman which has no beginning and end, no birth and death, no coming into being and going away. One observes charcoal fire to be straight or curved according to one's perception. However, the charcoal fire does not possess these attributes. Neither our mind produces the appearances nor does the appearances produce the mind. If one believes in cause and effect, one is constantly immersed in the cycle of existence, in *samsara*.

These views closely resemble the views of the Madhyamika school, enunciated in Nagarjuna's Karikas and the Sunyavada and Vijnanavada teachings.

Ramanuja

Ramanuja was born in Sriperumbudur, a suburb of Chennai, in 1077 and lived until 1157. He founded the Vishishtadvaita school, which differed from Shankara and Madhavacharya on the question of the relationship of the universal soul, Brahman, to the individual soul and matter. He is one of the most revered Vaishnavite saints even today.

It is said that his philosophical foundations were influenced by the Alwars of the Bhakti movement, who lived between the sixth and eighth centuries. The Alwars, however, composed their verses in Tamil while Ramanuja penned his texts in Sanskrit.

Ramanuja initially served as a priest in a temple in Kanchipuram. His guru was Yadava Prakasa, who adhered to the Advaita Vedanta tradition. Ramanuja disagreed with his guru later and became a disciple of Yamunacharya.

As opposed to Shankara's prescription that knowledge of the Brahman will lead to moksha, Ramanuja stressed the bhakti aspect and devotion to a personal god as the path to liberation.

There are unconfirmed stories that Ramanuja was persecuted by the Chola king Adhirajendra for his Vaishnavite beliefs and had to find sanctuary in the court of the Hoysala king in Karnataka.

Ramanuja denied that Brahman is the only reality and that all the objects in the universe are just an illusion. According to him, Brahman was composed of both unconscious matter (*achit*) and finite spirits (*chit*). Agreeing with the Saankhya view of the conception of the world, Ramanuja says that unconscious matter is prakriti, an uncreated, eternal reality. At the same time, Ramanuja differs from Saankya thought in the sense that this prakriti is controlled by Brahman (god) just as the soul controls the body. All knowledge and the world's objects are true. At the time of *pralaya*, the destruction and reconstruction of the world, the original undifferentiated matter transforms into three kinds of elements – fire, water and earth. These elements possess the qualities of *sattva*, *rajas* and *tamas*. Together, they form the basis of the millions of objects that we perceive in the world.

Ramanuja comes closer to materialistic positions when he says that the creator and the creations are not illusions. As a corollary, all knowledge is true.

The Ramanuja philosophy takes a middle ground between Shankara's *advaita*, which holds that only Brahman is real and the external world is unreal and Madhava's later *dvaita* philosophy, which holds that the supreme self and the individual self and the world of objects are real and different from each other. Ramanuja posits that Brahman is the only reality in the world, like Shankara, but Brahman contains within itself the material objects as well as the finite souls, which are also real. During *pralaya*, before the creation of a new universe, the parts within Brahman are undifferentiated. Brahman contains only pure matter and bodyless souls in an unmanifested form. When the universe was created, Brahman was manifested as the world of objects and individual souls. But Brahman does not undergo change or get subjected to the miseries and pleasures of life.

In Ramanuja's view, God has qualities (*saguna*), such as being omnipotent, omniscient and benevolent.

Madhava's Dvaita Philosophy

Madhava's Dvaita Vedanta holds the view that there are two separate realities in the world. The first and independent reality is Brahman, god, and in particular, Vishnu. In this, Madhava's Brahman resembles the monotheistic god of other religions. This supreme reality is eternal, all-knowing and compassionate.

The second dependent reality is the universe comprising the soul, body and matter. Unlike the god of the Advaita Vedanta, the god of Dvaita Vedanta exercises a personal role and governs and controls all that is happening in the universe. God has personal traits (*saguna*), and Vishnu is the god as distinct from the devas, who are souls that have reached a higher level, but mortal nevertheless, and dependent on the supreme being.

Moksha (liberation) can be attained once the realization dawns that Vishnu is the ultimate reality and all indivi dual souls are dependent on him. An essential part of Dvaita philosophy is Bhakti Yoga.

The Life of Madhavacharya

Madhava (1199–1278) was the principal proponent of the Dvaita school of Vedanta. He termed his philosophy as Tatvavada (discussions or arguments from a realistic point of view).

He lived in Karnataka near Udipi. Very early in his life, he became a sanyasi and studied the classics of Indian philosophy. His commentaries on the Upanishads, Brahma Sutras and the Bhagavat Gita are considered excellent works. He was a prolific writer, authoring thirty-seven Sanskrit works. Perhaps most prominent among them is the Anuvyakhyana, which accompanies his *bhashya* on Brahma Sutra as a philosophical supplement. It is considered a masterpiece.

He was an ardent critic of both Shankara's Advaita and Ramanuja's Vishishta Advaita schools of thought. He travelled extensively, engaging scholars in philosophical debates.

Madhava's dvaita outlook holds that the Brahman, the ultimate reality, and the *atman*, the individual self, are two independent realities. According to him, moksha could be achieved only through the grace of god. Madhava's dvaita variety of Vedanta is among the three most influential schools of Vedanta.

Madhava's Dvaita philosophy acknowledges the existence of categories shown in the figure. There are twenty different substances. All the twenty-four qualities of the Vaisheshika school are acknowledged and a few more. For want of space here, we will not be able to go into a detailed description of the categories and their constituent members.

The Madhava school admits that there are three valid sources of knowledge (*pramanas*) in contrast to one in Charvaka and six in Advaita schools. They are perception (*pratyaksha*), inference (*anumana*) and testimony (*shabda*).

Categories

- Substance (*dravya*)
- Quality (*guna*)
- Action (*karma*)
- Class character (*samanvaya*)
- Particularity (*vishesha*)
- Qualified (*vishishta*)
- Whole (*amshi*)
- Power (*shakti*)
- Similarity (*sadrashya*)
- Negation (*abhava*)

Self-Validity of Knowledge

We discussed the concept of self-validity of knowledge in the chapter on Mimansa. In the Madhava system, we are introduced to an intuitive agent called sakshi, which ascertains that the knowledge is valid. Sakshi is an intelligent and conscious agent that assists in perception across space and distance. If there is a doubt that the perception may be clouded by a defect that may lead to an error, then sakshi suspends its judgement. When there is a possibility of error, then sakshi remains inactive. But the *manas*, driven by the passion of attachment, makes a wrong judgement. It confuses illusion with reality.

Perception is of two types. The first is external perception, which arises from the interaction of the five senses with the world of objects, and the second is internal perception, which arises from the inner sense, the mind.

Inference means the acquiring of knowledge from one or more observations and based on previous confirmed truths. For example, concluding that there must be a fire when observing smoke.

Testimony relies on knowledge gathered from reliable authorities, past and present.

> **The Changing Status of Prakriti**
>
> In the early Saankhya period, *prakriti* meant primordial matter and *purusha* meant consciousness or the soul.
>
> While *purusha* became equated to the soul over time, the original meaning was the male human body. *Prakriti* was also described as the female principle. Female characteristics were attributed to the word.
>
> Gaudapada, the Advaita Vedanta scholar, when commenting on Saankhya Karika, mentioned that Saankhya believes that creation resulted from the union of the *purusha* and *prakriti*.
>
> In the early stages of Indian philosophy, *prakriti*, primeval matter, was considered as the first cause of the universe. *Purusha* had a minor role.
>
> By the time Vedanta philosophy developed, *purusha* was elevated to the status of the supreme ultimate reality, the Brahman.
>
> In Madhava's Dvaita conception, prakriti is the material cause of the material world. It is called maya, the consort of god. Though prakriti is all that is material and evolving, it is fully under the control of god. It may even be regarded as his will or strength (*shakti*).

> **Eternal Differences in Dvaita**
>
> According to Dvaita, the nature of the universe can be explained through five differences.
>
> These differences are fundamental, eternal and real. They are:
>
> i) Between the individual souls and god
>
> ii) Between matter (inanimate, insentient) and god
>
> iii) Between individual souls themselves
>
> iv) Between matter and the individual soul
>
> v) Between various types of matter.

Differences between the three Vedanta Schools

	Advaita	Vishishtadvaita	Dvaita
Founder	Shankara	Ramanuja	Madhava
Reality	Brahman is the only reality, and the world is illusory (*maya*).	God alone exists, but there is a plurality of souls.	Brahman and *atman* are two different entities, and *bhakti* is the route to eternal salvation.
Liberation	Ignorance of the reality is what causes suffering. Liberation can be obtained only by true knowledge of Brahman. Both the individual self (*atman*) and Brahman are the same, and knowing this difference causes liberation.	The study of scriptures alone is not sufficient. Intense devotion to god is necessary.	Intense devotion to Vishnu.

Form of Brahman	*Nirguna*	*Nirguna* and *saguna*	*Saguna*
Pramanas	*Pratyaksa* (perception), *anumana* (inference), *shabda* (verbal testimony), *upamana* (comparison), *arthapatti* (presumption) and *anupalabdi* (non-apprehension).	Perception, inference and testimony.	Perception, inference and testimony.

Key Takeaways

- Indian schools of philosophy accept one or more of the six *pramanas* as correct means of accurate knowledge and truths: i) *pratyakṣa* (perception), ii) *anumaṇa* (inference), iii) *upamaṇa* (comparison and analogy), iv) *arthapatti* (postulation, derivation), v) *anupalabdi* (non-perception, negative/cognitive proof) and vi) *shabda* (word, testimony of past or present reliable experts).
- Vedanta philosophy concerns itself with the elaboration of the philosophy contained in the Upanishads, which has been summarized in the Brahma Sutras authored by Badarayana.
- Upanishad means sitting near the teacher in order to overcome ignorance.
- Since the Upanishads form the tail end of the literature connected with the Vedas, its philosophy is called Uttara Mimansa.
- Badarayana's Brahma Sutra systematized the writings and presented a cogent view of the philosophy residing in the various Upanishads.
- The main idea presented by Shankara's Advaita Vedanta school is that the ultimate and absolute truth is the Brahman. It may appear as different selves, and these different selves may experience a world of many objects, but these are illusory.

- Ramanuja was the proponent of one of the three most influential philosophies based on the Vedanta school of thought, the *Vishishtadvaita* (qualified non-dualism).
- Ramanuja's philosophical outlook was greatly influenced by the works of the Alwars, the Tamil Bhakti saints.
- Madhava's Dvaita Vedanta holds the view that there are two separate realities in the world. The first and independent reality is Brahman, god, and in particular, Vishnu. The second dependent reality is the universe, comprising the soul, body and matter.
- The Madhava school admits that there are three valid sources of knowledge (*pramanas*).

Fact Check (Answers at the Back)

1. Indian schools of philosophy accept one or more of the six pramanas as the correct means of accurate knowledge. (Yes, No)
2. The Charvaka school accepts perception and inference as valid sources of knowledge. (Yes, No)
3. Shankara criticized Saankhya philosophy vehemently. (Yes, No)
4. Shankara was the proponent of the Dvaita system of philosophy. (Yes, No)
5. Gaudapada is the author of the Mandukya Karika, which was a commentary on the Mandukya Upanishad. (Yes, No).
6. The three most influential philosophies based on the Vedanta are Shankara's Advaita, Ramanuja's Vishishtadvaita and Madhavacharya's Dvaita. (Yes, No)
7. What was Shankara's approach towards the interpretation of Upanishads in contrast to the Mimansists?
   a. Shankara believed that Upanishads were not philosophical texts, unlike the Mimansists, who considered them as guides for conducting rituals.
   b. Shankara argued that Upanishads were mandatory injunctions for all individuals, while the Mimansists believed they were meant only for the wise.

c. Shankara interpreted the Upanishads as a path to salvation through knowledge of Brahman, which was contrary to the Mimansists' view that the Upanishads were only for material benefit seekers.
d. Shankara and the Mimansists agreed on the interpretation of the Upanishads as fundamental texts focusing on conducting rituals for worldly gains.

8. Ramanuja was the founder of:
   a. Advaita
   b. Vishishtadvaita
   c. Dvaita
   d. Achintya Bheda Abheda.
9. The Madhava school believes that the only reality is the universal soul, Brahman. (Yes, No)
10. The Madhava school believes there are four valid sources of knowledge. (Yes, No)

13

Bhagavat Gita: A New Philosophy and Code of Ethics

The Bhagavat Gita is a sacred Hindu scripture. It contains 700 verses and constitutes Chapters 23–40 of Book 6 of the Mahabharata, called the Bhishma Parva.

The Gita can be roughly dated to the second half of the first millennium BCE.

The Gita is set in the background of a dialogue between Pandava prince Arjuna and his guide and charioteer Krishna. The war between the Pandavas and the Kauravas is about to start. When seeing his kin and teachers in the opposite ranks, Arjuna is caught in a moral and emotional dilemma about the impending death and destruction. Inclined to walk out of the war, he seeks Krishna's counsel. The dialogue and discourse between Krishna and Arjuna form the body of the Gita.

> **Eternal Differences in Dvaita**
>
> Shankara, as expected, attempts to view the Gita from the point of his philosophy. He explains that the Gita decries rituals and sacrifices as recommended by the scriptures and instead emphasizes on right knowledge to attain salvation. Performing rituals is not a crime, but after attaining knowledge, if a person continues to perform rituals, then his actions are inconsistent since the two don't go together. For the wise man, there is no karma accumulated from past deeds. Vedic duties are required only for the ignorant.

In short, Krishna exhorts Arjuna to fulfil his Kshatriya duty and uphold dharma through karma. The dialogue touches upon the teachings of different schools of thought and ethical issues.

It is a period of the destruction of kinship-based clans and the rise of kingdoms. A new philosophy and code of ethics are required for the time, and the Gita attempts to do it.

In the Gita, Arjuna asks:

> *If, according to thy opinion, knowledge be superior to action, why, then, dost thou urge me to engage in an undertaking so dreadful as this?* (Gita, III.1)

Arjuna is perplexed that Krishna wants him to go ahead with the war, which is sure to result in huge losses of lives.

Krishna replies:

> *It hath before been observed by me that in this world there is a twofold rule of life, that of the Saankhyas by devotion of knowledge, and that of the Yogis by devotion of action.*
>
> *The man enjoyeth not freedom from action by abstaining from action, nor doth he obtain perfection from a total inactivity. No one ever resteth a moment inactive. Every man is involuntarily urged to act by those gunas which are inherent in his nature*[1].

Here, Shankara differs diametrically from the Gita. The Gita asserts that even wise men, even if it be god himself, have to perform duties but without expectations .

Yamunacharya (early tenth century), the teacher of Ramanuja (1077–1157), who taught Vedanta philosophy after Shankara, opines that the Gita establishes Vishnu as the highest Brahman. Salvation, that is merging with the Brahman, can be achieved through devotion (*bhakti*), which in turn requires the completion of one's caste duties, attaining right knowledge and giving up worldly pleasures.

The first six chapters of the Gita concentrate predominantly on the Yoga philosophy of attaining self-knowledge and self-concentration through knowledge and action. The next six chapters are concerned with Bhakti Yoga, the process of attainment of devotion through knowledge and action. The last six chapters relate to the later Saankhya philosophy of the *purusha* and *prakriti* and a supreme being.

The Gita explains that the self is immortal, that man should perform his caste duties in a detached manner without worrying about the fruits of his actions since those are not the actions of the self, and that it is the three *gunas* that are responsible for man's actions.

Key Takeaways

- The Bhagavat Gita is considered a sacred text in Hinduism, widely revered and quoted in various cultural and religious contexts.
- Early commentaries, such as Shankara's Gita Bhashya, interpret the Gita from specific philosophical viewpoints, with Shankara emphasizing the superiority of knowledge over ritual action for achieving salvation.
- The Gita presents a twofold path to spiritual freedom: through knowledge (as advocated by the Saankhyas) and through action (as followed by the yogis), arguing against inactivity and highlighting that actions driven by inherent qualities (*gunas*) are unavoidable.
- It diverges from Shankara's interpretation by suggesting that even wise men and deities must perform duties, but without attachment to the outcomes, thereby not accruing karma.
- The text is structured around themes of self-knowledge, devotion (*bhakti*), and understanding of the universe through the lens of Yoga, Saankhya and Vedanta philosophies, ultimately teaching that performing one's societal roles in a detached manner leads to spiritual liberation.

Fact Check (Answers at the Back)

1. Which philosophical stance does Shankara take in his commentary on the Bhagavat Gita?
   a. He emphasizes the importance of rituals and sacrifices as essential for salvation.
   b. He views right knowledge as superior to and a replacement for rituals and sacrifices in achieving salvation.
   c. He believes in the continuation of performing rituals after attaining knowledge.
   d. He asserts that actions, not knowledge, are the primary means to attain salvation.
2. How does the Bhagavat Gita describe the path to spiritual freedom?
   a. By advocating for a life of total inactivity and withdrawal from the world.
   b. Through a strict adherence to performing rituals and sacrifices.
   c. Through a twofold rule of life, involving devotion to knowledge and devotion to action.
   d. By urging followers to focus only on accumulating wealth and earthly possessions.
3. What is the Bhagavat Gita's stance on performing duties and actions?
   a. It encourages action without any consideration for the morality of the act.
   b. It suggests that actions are not necessary for those who have attained wisdom.
   c. It advocates for performing duties in a detached manner, without focusing on the fruits of actions.
   d. It recommends ceasing all forms of physical and mental actions as a way to achieve enlightenment.

14

Tantra and Shaktism: Emphasis on the Female Principle

Little is known about the origins of Tantrism and its proponents. Its philosophical outlook and practices are shrouded in secrecy because Tantra was practised by a closed community of adherents. In a way, Tantra pervades all Indian systems of philosophy, and hence, may have ancient beginnings. Its general features include rituals, yogic practices, magical mantras and diagrams and sexual rites. Those who practised Tantric practices rigorously were believed to acquire supernatural powers, the equivalent of moksha in other philosophical systems[1].

> **Tantra philosophy could be said to have strongly influenced the Shaiva, Shakta and Pancharatra cults. It also influenced the Buddhist school.**

Texts belonging to various schools, such as Saankhya, Yoga, Mimansa and Vedanta, refer to Tantra in different contexts. Some scholars push the history of Tantra's origins to as early as the Vedas and early Saankhya philosophy. In the early medieval period (600–1200 CE), Tantra gained wide acceptance across regions and cults.

Taking on from the concept of the world evolving from the contact of the *purusha* and *prakriti*, Tantra considers evolution as caused by the union of masculine and feminine energy. Even today, *purusha* represents the male in most Indian languages. The Tantric school considers energy (*shakti*) as feminine. One who indulges in Tantric practices is said to perform *sadhana*. Disciples are initiated into the Tantra fold by a secret mantra uttered into the ears by a guru. Mantras (prayers), *yantras* (diagrams) and *mudras* (poses) play an important role in Tantric rituals. Yogic practices are also common in Tantra. An individual can attain union with the supreme power through Tantric practices when the energy called *kundalini*, which lies like a coiled serpent inside the body, uncoils itself. In most practices, sexual rites also form an important part, although they have been overstressed by Tantra's opponents. Tantra practices involve five elements, though it is not clear whether this is a concoction of opposing beliefs: *madha* (liquor), *mamsa* (meat), *matsya* (fish), *mudra* (parched grain) and *maithuna* (sexual union).

Followers of Tantrism worship Vishnu, Shiva and Shakti. Shaivism and Shaktism are closely related to Tantrism since Shiva and Shakti are considered to be the male and female principles of the supreme god. Among the followers of Vishnu, the Pancharatra sect was closely related to Tantrism. There were also other sects, such as the Kapalikas and the Kalamukhas, who were also practising Tantrists.

In a way, the practices of Tantric-related cults such as the Kalamukhas and others were an expression of their opposition to upper-caste rituals. These cults were also popular among the tribal peoples, who were unaccustomed to Vedic practices. Such cults were later slowly integrated into the mainstream fold by syncretizing their gods with the Hindu pantheon.

Even though Tantrism followed beliefs and practices not in line with Vedic orthodoxy, it became popular throughout the Indian subcontinent, influencing Tibetan religious practices, too. It differed from Vedic practices in the sense that it included people of all castes, as well as women. It gave special importance to goddesses, as evident in the religious text *Devi Mahatmya*. The goddesses had a personality of their own and did not function just as consorts of male gods. Goddess-worshipping cults were probably matrilineal, and their followers presumably belonged to the lower strata of society. These cults were also closely aligned with fertility rites and sexual rites, considered taboo in orthodox societies. Women in these societies practised much larger roles as priestesses and gurus, running their own ashrams, and as poets, as evident in the Tamil Bhakti movement[2].

Figure 16: *Sri Laxmi Yantra*

While Tantrism has been criticized for its unorthodox activities by other schools of thought, it was an effective outlet for expressing opposition to the brahminical order of society.

Tantric ideas are also reflected in Vajrayana Buddhism. Similar to the Shakti cult, the spouses of the male bodhisattvas, called Taras, were the object of veneration among followers.

Scholars such as Debiprasad have expressed the view that Tantrism was practised in early agricultural communities where women had a higher social status, and magical rites were common[3]. He has attempted to trace the origins of the Mother Goddess in Indian civilization to the female figurines found in the sites of the Harappan civilization[4].

Shaktism

In both the Tantra and Saankhya schools, the female principle or *prakriti* the source of all activity, the coming and going of all products and phenomena, etc. This view is the reflection of societies where females had supremacy in many aspects of economic and social life, such as in agricultural economies. The female principle assumes importance in matriarchal societies. In early agricultural societies – since agriculture was the discovery of women and where even today it remains their exclusive preoccupation in the countryside – conditions were ripe for establishing the economic and social supremacy of the female. In the philosophical sphere, schools or trends like Lokayata, Saankhya, Tantra and Shakta, the emphasis is on the female principle (*prakriti pradhanya*). Other schools, by contrast, emphasize the male principle (*purusha pradhanya*).[5]

There is evidence that the female principle was dominant in many non-Vedic tribes, while the Vedic people, belonging to a pastoral economy, held the male, purusha, as supreme. The Purusha Sukta, a section of the later parts of the Rig Veda, exalts the purusha in this verse:

> *A thousand heads hath purusha, a thousand eyes, a thousand feet.*
> *On every side pervading earth he fills a space ten fingers wide.*
> *This purusha is all that yet hath been and all that is to be.*
> *The lord of immortality which waxes greater still by food.*
> *So mighty is his greatness; yea, greater than this is purusha.*
> *All creatures are one-fourth of him, three-fourths eternal life in heaven.*
> *With three-fourths purusha went up: one-fourth of him again was here.*
> *Thence he strode out to every side over what eats not and what eats.*[6]

Among the material remains of Mohenjo-Daro and Harappa, a large number of terracotta female figurines were discovered. It is speculated that such figurines represent the mother goddess or the nature goddess. Such figures have been found not only in the Harappan civilization regions but also in many other early societies. It is reasonable to suppose that these figurines were prevalent in matriarchal societies. In India, the idea of the mother goddess did not end with the Harappan civilization. To this day, there are many female deities and *gramadevatas* (village goddesses) in India. Female deities are still predominant in Indian society and have their independent existence, such as Durga, Kali, Chandi, Kottravai and others. The survival of peasant and tribal societies in India provides the material basis for the worship of such female goddesses.

The worship of female goddesses is usually associated with fertility rites, which again, is very prevalent in India today. As early as the first millennium, the Puranas compiled a list of goddesses, portraying them as different forms of the female principle. These goddesses, such as Katyayani, Kanyakumari and Durga, became associated with Shakti worship.

The Mahabharata has hymns in praise of Durga and addresses her by various names. The goddess is also described as associated with forests, rivers, animals and other branches of nature. The epic mentions the names of some tribes who worship Durga. She is described as a goddess to be feared, personifying death and fond of wine, meat and sacrifice. She is spoken of as the saviour of the universe.

Another significant work that extols Shakti or Devi is the Devi Mahatmya, a part of the Markandeya Purana, written around the seventh century BCE. In this, there are stories of how the goddess slayed demons who were harassing the gods. One of the stories is related to the famous Mahishasuramardini (the slayer of Mahishasura), whose praise is sung even today. Many Durga images belonging to the early centuries of the first millennium have been unearthed around Mathura and Sonkh[7].

Similarities between Tantra and Saankhya[8]

Some scholars have advanced the opinion that the Saankhya principles of purusha and prakriti contributed to the theory of Tantrism. According to them, this theory is about the union of the soul of the universe (*purusha*) with primordial matter (*prakriti*).

Others believe that Tantrism is even more ancient and that it gave supreme importance to the principle of *prakriti*. Both Tantrism and Saankhya were strongly opposed to the viewpoint of a supreme god. Saankhya was often called the 'nirishwara pradhana karana vada', which meant the 'godless doctrine of primordial matter'. The Saankhya system was among the first Indian philosophical schools to put forward a theory of matter, a theory of causality, a theory of knowledge and a theory of evolutionary process. While Tantrism may be older, the Saankhya system gave it a philosophical underpinning. Shankara has characterized Saankhya philosophy as the 'Tantra of Kapila'.

Key Takeaways

- Tantra is a complex and secretive tradition that integrates rituals, yogic practices, mantras and sexual rites pervading all Indian systems of philosophy with ancient origins and aiming at the acquisition of supernatural powers or moksha.
- It has significantly influenced various religious cults and practices across India, including Shaivism, Shaktism, the Pancharatra sect, and Vajrayana Buddhism, promoting the worship of deities such as Vishnu, Shiva and Shakti and emphasizing the union of masculine and feminine energies.

- Despite its unorthodox practices, Tantrism offered an inclusive spiritual path beyond Vedic orthodoxy, welcoming all castes and genders, and played a role in social opposition against the Brahmanical order, thereby contributing to the syncretic evolution of Indian religious and cultural landscapes.
- The emphasis on the female principle or *prakriti* as the source of the universe and all activity is central in both Tantra and Saankhya schools, reflecting societies where women had significant economic and social supremacy, particularly in agricultural contexts.
- The worship of female deities has deep roots in Indian spiritual and societal life, manifesting in a wide array of goddesses associated with fertility, nature and strength and remains a vibrant part of Indian tradition, showing the enduring legacy of matriarchal influences in spiritual practices.

Fact Check (Answers at the Back)

1. What is a key aspect of Tantric practices?
   a. Strict adherence to Vedic rituals without any inclusion of yogic practices or mantras.
   b. The pursuit of supernatural powers or moksha through a variety of practices, including rituals, yogic exercises and the use of mantras and sexual rites.
   c. Complete rejection of all forms of physical and spiritual practices in favour of philosophical debates.
   d. Exclusive focus on meditation without any rituals, mantras or sexual rites.
2. How did Tantrism influence the religious and cultural landscape of India?
   a. By maintaining strict adherence to Vedic practices and excluding all non-Vedic elements.
   b. Through its secretive and exclusive practices, which were accessible only to a select few.

c. By offering an inclusive spiritual path that welcomed all castes and genders, influencing various cults and promoting the worship of deities like Vishnu, Shiva and Shakti.

d. By rejecting all forms of deity worship and focusing solely on atheistic philosophical discourse.

3. What is the significance of the female principle or prakriti in the Tantra and Saankhya schools of thought?

   a. It denotes male dominance in agricultural societies.

   b. It is considered a minor aspect that has little to no impact on the cosmos.

   c. It is regarded as the source of the universe and all activity, reflecting societies with female economic and social supremacy.

   d. It is solely associated with weakness and passiveness in the cosmos.

15

Ayurveda: Body, Soul and Mind

The medical schools of ancient India had thinkers, too, who were fully conversant with speculations of the philosophic schools and contributed to their further enrichment. Medicine was an advanced physical science in India. The texts of the medical schools reflect a new way of life, and their interpretation of the relationship between the body, soul and mind is of interest to scholars of philosophy.

Timeline of
Ayurveda

Roughly between **100 BCE and 150–200 CE**	Charaka
Sushruta	**7th or 6th century CE**
Between **4th century BCE to 6th century CE**	*Charaka Samhita*
Chakrapani Dutta	**1060 CE**
12th century CE	Dalhana

The Ayurveda system of medicine has survived for more than 2000 years and is a popularly sought-after treatment method even today. The most authentic texts related to this medical system are the *Charaka Samhita* and the *Sushruta Samhita*.

Some scholars believe that Ayurveda is related to the Atharva Veda. Charaka says that it is a subsection of the Atharva Veda (which deals with curatives and charms) and originally consisted of 100,000 verses. According to Charaka, the science of medicine had always existed and only its systematic arrangement into a *samhita*[1] was done at a later point in time. Some even considered Ayurveda as the fifth Veda. There is a view that Ayurveda cures people of diseases produced by bad diet and the Atharva Veda cures people who live a sinful and evil life[2].

Charaka Samhita

The *Charaka Samhita* was not written in one go. It had several authors contributing different layers at different times. The first layer may have been written as early as the third century BCE. There is proof that the Samhita was considered a medical authority by the first part of the fifth century CE. There is reason to believe that Agnivesha had written the earlier part of the text and Charaka had edited it. The text was again edited later by Dridhbala.

The corpus is divided into 120 chapters grouped into eight sections. The chapters deal with a variety of medical subjects such as diseases, diagnosis, therapy, nutrition, anatomy and philosophy.

Chakrapani Datta (1060 CE) made significant contributions to the Ayurveda system of medicine through his academic commentaries on the primary texts in the field.

Dalhana (twelfth century CE) wrote a commentary on the *Sushruta Samhita* called *Nibandha Sangraha*.

Philosophers such as Debiprasad believe that *Charaka Samhita* is older than *Saankhya Karika* of Ishwarakrishna. The two texts differ in their treatment of the Saankhya doctrine. It is probable that the discussion on Saankhya given by Charaka corresponds to an older school of Saankhya. Further, the passages in the Mahabharata that pertain to the exposition of Saankhya doctrines to King Janaka, the king of Mithila, are close to the Charaka version in their content[3].

Considering that there is a lot of reference to the philosophical ideas of the Saankhya, Yoga and Vaisheshika schools in its texts, the Ayurveda school deserves a separate chapter in this book for discussion.

> **Sushruta Samhita**
>
> Like the *Charaka Samhita*, the *Sushruta Samhita*, too, has been written by several authors over a long period. The first layer dealing with surgery was composed probably just before the beginning of the common era. It went through several edits till the fifth century CE.
>
> The Samhita has six sections covering topics such as symptoms, pathology, medicine, medical training, surgery, removal of splinters, anatomy and philosophy.

Source of Morbidity

The health of the body is determined by two kinds of qualities – the *mala*, denoting substances that weaken the body, and *prasada*, which purify the body of toxins.

Central to the theory of Ayurveda are the three *doshas* – *vayu* or *vata* (air), *pitta* (bile) and *kapha* (phlegm) – which are the source of all morbidities. The *doshas* are part of the *malas*. So long as they remain in balance, the body is without disease. They are a part of *dhatus*, constituents in the body that are always there but which need to be balanced.

Among the three *doshas*, *vayu* is concentrated in the intestine, *pitta* in the stomach and *kapha* in the chest. Other waste products are sweat, urine, excreta and even blood and semen. The body fluids traverse the body through a complicated network of ducts, similar to the veins of a leaf, carrying nutrition to all parts of the body.

Mind, Soul and Senses

The philosophical ideas of Ayurveda stem from those of the Nyaya and Vaisheshika schools. But there are adaptations as well.

The two schools consider *manas*, the mind organ, as a separate sense, a special type of sense but a sense, nevertheless. Ayurveda, on the other hand, believes that since *manas* is not like the ordinary senses and it cannot acquire knowledge the way other senses do, it is then a category that transcends the ordinary senses.

In Ayurveda, the self is the permanent subject of all acts of consciousness. It makes the first effort. When the manas comes into contact with objects, whether physical objects such as a jug or mental objects such as pain and pleasure, the self makes an effort to investigate or grasp the meaning of these physical or mental objects. It moves the manas, which, in turn, moves the senses until the self acquires knowledge of the objects to its satisfaction.

The senses that *manas* moves are constituted of the five elements of ether, air, light, water and earth.

Though all the senses are made up of the five elements, a particular sense organ is associated with a particular element because of the preponderance of that element in it. Therefore, the elements are associated with sense organs and chakras (wheels for energy points in the body) this way:

1. Ether (ears, hearing) (throat)
2. Air (skin, touch) (heart)
3. Fire (eyes, seeing) (navel)
4. Water (tongue, taste buds, taste) (sacral)
5. Earth (nose, smell) (root)

The sense cognitions are produced by the self/soul, manas and the senses and the sense objects acting together.

According to Charaka, the soul, mind and body are connected like the three corners of a tripod.

The self is viewed in two ways in Ayurveda. When the self is in contact with manas and the senses, then it enters the sphere of change and consciousness. In its subtler state, it is eternal and unchangeable and has cognition of all its past and future states. In this view, the Ayurveda school differs from some other schools of thought.

Yet, in general, the *Charaka Samhita* agrees with the Vaisheshika outlook. It enumerates the Vaisheshika categories but does not stick to the same interpretation. It repeats the five elements, manas, time, space, self, *gunas*, buddhi (intelligence) and so on with some departures. (See the chapter on Nyaya philosophy).

Sushruta Samhita starts with a faithful description of Saankhya principles, but there are deviations in their interpretation.

Sources of Acquiring Knowledge

The practitioner of Ayurveda requires a keen sense of observation and coming to conclusions using logical reasoning. According to Ayurveda, objects (in this case diseases) can be existent (*sat*) or non-existent (*asat*). There are four valid means of investigation, including perception (*pratyaksha*), inference (*anumana*), logical reasoning (*yukti*) and testimony (*aptopadesha*).

In the case of testimonial evidence, the person whose testimony is considered should be free from rajas and tamas, have a preponderance of sattva and have extensive insights into the past, present and future.

Perception is obtained because of the coordination of the self, senses, manas and the sense objects. Knowledge obtained through sense contact is valid knowledge through perception. While pleasure and pain do not need sense contact, they are, nevertheless, considered valid knowledge through perception.

Yukti is not considered a separate *pramana* by other schools of thought, but Charaka argues that it helps knowledge gathering, like forecasting a good harvest from conditions such as rains, quality of seeds, etc.

Conducting Medical Debates

Indian medical practitioners used logic not only in diagnosing an ailment but also in debates involving the selection of the right treatment method from many choices. Thus, these practitioners were not only supposed to be good at observation and inference but also in presenting their views skillfully in a dispute.

The earliest texts available, where the principles of debating have been systematically compiled, are strangely those connected with the medical schools of Charaka and Sushruta.

In the third part of the *Charaka Samhita*, called 'Vimana Sthana', we find a discussion on the principles of debating. The chapter also deals with other topics, such as the training and ethics of medical practitioners.

Charaka encourages a lot of discussion (*sambhasha*) and knowledge sharing to gain proficiency in debates and arrive at the truth. The discussions can be friendly or hostile. In friendly discussions, there is an atmosphere of give and take and forgiving each other's mistakes.

Handling hostile disputes requires a lot of finesse, and Charaka has a lot to say about this. Before launching oneself into a hostile discussion, a person should check out whether the opponent is inferior or superior to him, whether the assembly is learned or ignorant, friendly, neutral or hostile. An opponent must be judged not only on his intellectual capacity but also on his moral bearing. A hostile assembly must be avoided at all costs. A debater has a chance to win in an ignorant, friendly or neutral assembly by being tactical. If the opponent is not a well-known intellectual, he can be worn down by long quotes from the sutras or wit and satire. If the opponent is equal, then the debater should identify his weak spot, target his attacks there and discredit him.

> **Syllogistic Reasoning**
>
> Thesis: The *purusha* is eternal
>
> Reason (*hetu*): Because it is uncreated
>
> Example (*drshtantha*): The sky is uncreated, and it is eternal
>
> Similarity (*upanayah*): Just as the sky is uncreated, so the purusha is also uncreated
>
> Establish the thesis (*nigamanam*): Therefore, the *purusha* is eternal

Charaka describes ten categories that need to be understood to attain mastery in Ayurveda. Among them are *kaarana* (the actor, physician), *karana* (the instrument, medicine), *karya* (the action, restoration of balance), *karya-phala* (the effect, happy state of body and mind), *desa* (place, patient), *kala* (season or day, condition of patient), and *pravritti* (the effort of the physician).

Sushruta enumerates thirty-two technical terms or maxims that can help physicians score a point over their hostile critics.

It is a fact that for physicians – whose objective is to diagnose a disease, understand its causes and find a cure, scientific methods of investigation – logic, debate and discussion come naturally. A successful physician has to convince the patient, as well as his critics, about the method of treatment and argue confidently about its benefits. So the rules of debates and discussions mattered to physicians a lot. Since the art of debate has not been described in any earlier literature, it is reasonable to suppose that Charaka gathered all the methods of investigation, discussion, dispute resolution and logic into his work .

Key Takeaways

- There are many references to the philosophical ideas of the Saankhya, Yoga and Vaisheshika schools in the Ayurvedic text *Charaka Samhita*.
- Central to the theory of Ayurveda are the three *doshas* – *vayu* (air), *pitta* (bile) and *kapha* (phlegm) – which are the source of all morbidities.
- The philosophical ideas of Ayurveda stem from those of the Nyaya and Vaisheshika schools. But there are adaptations as well.
- In Ayurveda, the self is the permanent subject of all acts of consciousness.
- According to Charaka, the soul, *manas* and body are connected like the three corners of a tripod.
- Ayurveda acknowledges four valid means of investigation, including perception (*pratyaksha*), inference (*anumana*), logical reasoning (*yukti*) and testimony (*aptopadesha*).
- Acquiring knowledge through valid means of investigation, logic, debates and settling disputes are a vital part of a physician's life.
- The Ayurvedic schools compiled the principles of debating systematically.
- *Vada*, *jalpa* and *vithanda* are three kinds of ways to debate or settle disputes.

Fact Check (Answers at the Back)

1. The Ayurvedic system is a medical school and is not connected with philosophical ideas. (Yes, No)
2. The Charaka Samhita has borrowed philosophical ideas from the Nyaya and Vaisheshika schools. (Yes, No)
3. Ayurveda acknowledges three valid means of acquiring knowledge. (Yes, No)
4. The Charaka Samhita may be the earliest text to lay down the principles of debating and discussion. (Yes, No)

16

The Bhakti Movement: Devotion and Love

The philosophical ideas of these northern schools clashed with the ideas expressed in the Sangam poems, which may have been composed from the third century BCE onwards according to existing evidence. Just as the tribal societies of the north had transitioned to kingdoms with the spread of private property, which created inequalities in society, Tamil society also transitioned during the Sangam period. Several Tamil works – heroic and love poetry, works of grammar, didactic texts and epics – were produced during this period. Altogether, they constituted a huge corpus. While most of the texts were in verse or the form of aphorisms, they exhibited a variety of philosophical ideas characteristic of the region. There are no systematically compiled texts on various schools of thought in

Timeline of

Tamil Literature

2nd to 5th century CE	*Pattupattu (Ten Idylls)*
3rd or 5th century CE	*Ettutogai* (Eight anthologies)
100 BCE **5th century** CE	*Tholkappiyam (treatise on Tamil Grammar)*
5th to 6th century CE	*Silapthikaram (Tale of the Anklet)*
6th to 12th century CE	Tirumurai (holy scripture, Saivite canon)
5th to 10th century CE	*Nalayira Divya Prabandham* (4,000 holy hyumns, the Vaishnavite canon)
31 BCE **– 500** CE	Tiruvalluvar, author of *Tirukkural*

the south, but the texts reflected the philosophy and ethics of the prevailing society very well.

The Philosophy of Sangam Poetry

Early Sangam poetry is devoid of any references to Vedic or non-Vedic north Indian texts. The thought process in the poems, a kind of naturalism, is closer to that of the Harappan civilization and the Samhitas rather than that of the later schools of thought based on the Upanishads and the ascetic schools. The origin of the world is not attributed to any supreme creator but to the First Principle – nature, land and seasons.

The grammar book, *Tholkappiyam*, having established this, describes the five landscapes and the five seasons. The five landscapes are: i) *kurinji* (the mountainous region), ii) *mullai* (the forest region), iii) *marutham* (the riverine region), iv) *neythal* (the coastal region), and v) *palai* (the desert region). The classification is not to do with the geography of the region but the occupation, culture and ethos of people living in these regions. Though gods are affiliated with these landscapes, they do not have supernatural powers; neither are they creators of these landscapes. In real life, however, these five worlds did not exist in watertight compartments. People travelled from one landscape to another, and there was trade and commerce between these regions. But each region gave rise to its own thought process and world outlook. This can be called proto-materialism, somewhat akin to that of early tribal clans of the Vedic people.

Overlaid on these geographical landscapes are time, season, flora and fauna, which further shaped the ethics, morality, attitude and beliefs of the people. Man is a part of nature, not the centre of the universe.

The cosmology of the Sangam period is similar to that of the Vedic period in that the universe is believed to be made up of the five elements – land, sky, air, water and fire.

> **There is no reference in early Sangam literature to the self or soul, the cycle of birth and rebirth, transmigration and the idea of salvation from the world of sorrow.**

In the late or post-Sangam period, we see the growing influence of the schools of Ajivika, Jainism, Buddhism, Lokayata and Saankhya. Epics such as *Silapathikaram*, *Manimekalai*, *Seevaga Sinthamani* and *Neelakesi* and didactic works such as *Tirukkural* and *Naladiyar* were produced during this period. These schools had such far-reaching influence that Vedic orthodox schools remained in the shade. Just as in the north in earlier centuries, the Shramanic schools gained popularity in the south in an environment of the breaking down of kinship structures and tribal communities, state formation, expansion of trade and industry and growth of private property. The Shramanic philosophy was popular among migrants to cities, cut off from their kinship ties. They catered to the spiritual needs of the growing population of traders and craftsmen.

The literature in this period reflects a variety of behaviours, such as hedonism, asceticism, ethical conduct of household life, greed and war-mongering. Even though the influence of the ascetic sects is strong, Tamil literature does not strongly advocate asceticism. In essence, there is an emphasis on this-worldly aspects.

The Tamil Bhakti Movement

During the period from the late fifth century or early sixth to the ninth century, there arose a devotional movement in the Tamil region, spearheaded by the Vaishnavite Alwars and the Saivite Nayanars. The pantheon of Bhakti saints consisted of twelve Alwars and sixty-three Nayanars. The poems of the Alwars were compiled in the Nalayira Divya Prabandham (four thousand holy hymns) by Nadamuni. Those of the Nayanars were compiled into twelve volumes, into the *Tirumurai* (hymns) by Nambi Andar Nambi.

The Saivite Saint Manikkavachagar Sings:

Indra or Vishnu or Brahma

Their divine bliss carve not I

I seek the love of thy saints

Though my house perish thereby.

To the worst hell will I go

So but thy grace be with me

Best of all, how could my heart

Think of a God beside Thee?…

I had no virtue, penance, knowledge, self-control

A doll to turn

At other's will I danced, whistled fell.

But me He filled in every limb

With love's mad longing, and that I might climb

There whence there is no return.

(P. Kingsbury and G.E. Phillips, *Hymns of the Tamil Saivite Saints*, pp. 89, 127)

To some extent, the Bhakti sects were hostile to Buddhism and Jainism because of the anxiety of the Bhakti saints to win over followers to their fold. But they were, nevertheless, influenced by these schools.

The Bhakti sects were not formal in the sense that they did not enforce religious scriptures, rituals and sacrifices on their followers. While the saints themselves led ascetic lives, the followers were given a lot of scope to display their devotion and emotions in various ways.

In a way, the Bhakti movement was a people's movement given a religious form due to the conditions of the timc. Thc Bhakti saints questioned the inequality of the *varna* system and the stress on rituals and sacrifices by Vedic orthodoxy.

These sects encouraged temple worship through puja, involving an offering of flowers and fruits. This form of worship was accessible to all as compared to Vedic rituals, which were complicated and required priests for guidance.

While the preoccupation of some schools of thought was on emancipation through knowledge or rituals, the Bhakti movement propagated love for god and other human beings as the path to liberation. The emphasis was on a direct relationship with god without the need for an intermediary.

Like the unorthodox schools, the Bhakti movement allowed the entry of all castes and professions into their fold, including the untouchables. A few women also made their mark as Bhakti saints. The saints came from families engaged in carpentry, hunting, fishing, pottery and many other humble professions.

The basis of popularity of the Bhakti movement was similar to that of the Shramanic sects in the mid-first century BCE. It was a reaction to an oppressive Sanskritic culture that subordinated all castes to rituals and the *varna* system. The Bhakti poets also sang in the language of the masses, just as the Buddha and Mahavira got closer to the masses by using Pali.

The Bhakti movement was essentially materialist in the sense that it offered no promises of liberation from the cycle of birth through rituals and mantras. It did not preoccupy itself with metaphysical speculations about the soul, its relationship to the body, the impermanency of the world of objects, the effects of karma in a previous life and so on.

In a way, it was a product of the economic and political developments of the time. It opened the way to the upward mobility of groups of artisans and traders in the social hierarchy. It answered the spiritual needs of migrants from villages to cities, who were cut off from their kinship ties. It gave full play to the freedom offered by urbanization to new ideas and actions[1].

The Spread of the Bhakti Movement

The Tamil Bhakti movement inspired similar movements in neighbouring Karnataka, and then Maharashtra and other regions of India. Many poet-saints emerged as leaders of such movements, drawing lakhs of followers around them. They exhibited similar social reformist features, such as being inclusive and admitting women and people belonging to lower castes within their fold, rejecting rituals and sacrifices, and talking to the masses in their local dialects. The movements displayed a remarkable amount of diversity. Some sects believed in worshipping deities with attributes (*saguna*) such as Shiva and Vishnu, and others, without attributes (*nirguna*).

Leaders of the Bhakti Movement in Other Parts of India

Basavanna (1134–1196 CE)

Jnanadeva (c.1275–1296 CE)

Ramananda (c.1400–1476 CE)

Kabir (1398–1448 CE)

Guru Nanak (c.1469–1539 CE)

Mirabai (1498–1547 CE)

Sant Eknath (c.1533–1599 CE)

Tukaram (c.1608–1650 CE)

In Karnataka, Basavanna (1106–68 CE) led the Virashaiva or Lingayat movement. It attracted followers from many professions, such as artists, traders and farmers. The movement strongly voiced its views against Vedic orthodoxy, rituals, caste discrimination and superstition through verses called *vachanas*.

Akka Mahadevi is a well-known woman saint who belonged to this tradition. The followers of this tradition wear an image of the linga held with a necklace around their neck and do not believe in temple worship. They do not believe in funerary rites and rebirth and bury their dead instead of cremating them.

During the tenth and eleventh centuries, a mystic tradition called Sufism became popular in the Delhi Sultanate. It had features close to the Bhakti traditions in other parts of India. Arising from Islamic foundations, the Sufis spread the message of peace, harmony and love for god and the people, which resonated very well with large sections of the Indian people, particularly the most vulnerable. These thoughts and messages have survived over a thousand years. They were tolerant of non-Islamic traditions and open to syncretizing ideas from other schools of spirituality. The establishment of *khanqahs*, community centres or dormitories, built their credibility among other communities. These centres also served as community shelters for people from the lower castes. Their egalitarian outlook and spiritual and psychological guidance won them many adherents. Within the Sufi movement, the Chishti order, spearheaded by scholars such as Moinuddin Chishti, set up centres in many parts, such as Ajmer, which earned a considerable reputation in the region for their hospitality and charitable activities.

Tamil Didactic Poetry

There are a large number of works comprising hundreds of stanzas in Tamil poetry that have more philosophical and didactic value than as literature or poetry.

Prominent among these works is the compilation called the *Eighteen Shorter Texts*, known as *Patinenkilkanakku* in Tamil. Though they are works of the Sangam age, they find mention in the commentary by Perasiriyar in the thirteenth century. The reasons for the proliferation of such didactic literature may be due to many political and social reasons, as well as the impact of Buddhist and Jain philosophies on the Tamil intellect. Among the *Eighteen Shorter Texts* are eleven collections of maxims and aphorisms on rules of ethics or rules of public and private conduct. They are somewhat comparable to the Niti texts in Sanskrit which focus on ethical and moral principles.

Foremost among these didactic collections are the *Tirukkural* and the *Naladiyar*.

The *Tirukkural* is quite exceptional for its literary qualities, as well as its messages on ethics and aesthetics. It consists of 1,330 couplets divided into 133 sections of ten couplets each. The work relates to the moral and cosmic order, statesmanship, social ethics and other such topics. The author was most likely a Jain well-versed in poetry writing and with a knowledge of Sanskrit texts. He lived in Mylapore, a neighbourhood of present-day Chennai, between 400 and 500 CE. The ethics that the *Tirukkural* outlines are closer to Jain doctrines than others. But *Tiruvalluvar's* moral code is much more practical than the Jain code of conduct. The document has a single structural plan and is crafted by a single poet–philosopher. The entire book uses one metre called the *kuralvenpa*, having one metrical foot consisting of two or three metrical units. The 'terse, vivid couplets lend themselves so aptly to memorisation and quotation'. This is very true since many admirers in Tamil Nadu know all the verses by rote, and buses and government establishments display verses on boards and walls even today.

The Fusion of Bhakti Trends

In the fifteenth century, north India was the scene of a great mingling of philosophical streams flowing from the south Indian Bhakti movements with Sufism and Islam. It was spearheaded by Kabir and his teacher Ramananda. Kabir was born in 1440 near present-day Varanasi to Muslim parents. Ramananda was the forbearer of the Vedantic thoughts of the twelfth-century reformer Ramanuja in the south. As we have seen, the revival set in motion by the Bhakti saints of the south from the sixth century onwards was a reaction against the strict practices of Vedic orthodoxy. It was also a striving to replace the emphasis on scriptures, which were accessible only to a few, with the concept of a god accessible to all and practices that could be sustained by the ordinary masses.

Ramananda and Kabir lived at a time when the vibrant poetry and the earthy philosophy of Persian mystics and Sufi saints like Attar, Sadi, Jalaluddin Rumi and Hafiz were exerting their sway on vast swathes of the subcontinent. The genius of Ramananda and Kabir was reflected in their efforts to fuse these varied trends.

For years, Kabir was a close disciple of Ramananda, participating in theological and philosophical debates with mullahs and Brahmins alike. He shunned the life of an ascetic and despised bodily mortifications to attain liberation. He was a skilled musician and poet, drawing millions of ordinary people around him. At the same time, he was a family man and a weaver by profession. He was not a great scholar of scriptures but composed and sang his poems in the language of the masses. He called himself the 'child of Allah and Ram' and was considered a heretic because of his unorthodox ways of worship. He proclaimed that god was 'neither in Kaaba nor in Kailash.' It is believed that when the mullahs and priests of Varanasi appealed to Sultan Sikandar Lodi to give him the death sentence, the Sultan empathized with Kabir and ordered his banishment from the city.

Kabir is said to have influenced Guru Nanak, the founder of the Sikh religion, through his poems on compassion and love for human beings. His verses find a place in the Adi Granth, the Sikh scripture. His verses constitute the largest contribution from a non-Sikh poet.

Key Takeaways

- The migration of philosophical ideas from the north to the south of the Indian subcontinent may have started as early as the fourth century BCE.
- The composition of Sangam poems is estimated to have started in the third century BCE.
- The Sangam texts were not categorized according to philosophical categories but reflected the philosophical thoughts of the period.
- The thought process in the Sangam poems, a kind of naturalism, is closer to that of the Harappan civilization and Samhitas rather than that of the later schools of thought based on the Upanishads and ascetic schools.
- In the late or post-Sangam period, we see the growing influence of the schools of Ajivika, Jainism, Buddhism, Lokayata and Saankhya.
- The Bhakti movement propagated love for god and other human beings as the path to liberation. The emphasis was on a direct relationship with god without the need for an intermediary.
- The Bhakti movement was essentially materialist in the sense that it offered no promises of liberation from the cycle of birth through rituals and mantras but emphasized love for fellow human beings and social inclusion.
- The Tamil Bhakti movement inspired the spread of Bhakti philosophy to other regions.
- There are a large number of works comprising hundreds of stanzas in Tamil poetry that have more philosophical and didactic value than as literature or poetry.

Fact Check (Answers at the Back)

1. The philosophical underpinnings of the Sangam period were similar to those of the Upanishads. (Yes, No)
2. The Tamil Bhakti movement considered rituals and sacrifices as the path to liberation. (Yes, No)
3. The Tamil Bhakti saints composed their works in Sanskrit. (Yes, No)
4. The Tamil Bhakti sects encouraged temple worship through puja as opposed to Vedic rituals and sacrifices. (Yes, No)
5. The Tirukkural is a didactic work on ethics and aesthetics. (Yes, No)

Conclusion

Many philosophers of the colonial period expressed the view that Indian philosophy was not made up of rigorous systems of thought but consisted mainly of mythological tales and ethical teachings.

We have seen that most of the schools of Indian thought emerged sometime between 600 to 200 BCE. It is difficult to arrange them in chronological order since there are differences of opinion on which system came first. The systems underwent a lot of changes from crude outlines at the beginning to more evolved structures. This process went on until the seventeenth century CE, after which further development stopped literally. This may be considered as one reason for the inundation of Western thought.

We have discussed Indian philosophy over a period of 4000 years if we include the Harappan civilization. Though the schools of philosophy continued to exist for at least 2600 years, their world outlook and philosophical viewpoints could not have remained stagnant and unaffected by material changes like the expansion of trade, gathering pace of urbanization, growth of industry and other factors. Accordingly, philosophical thoughts changed to suit the new conditions.

We have so far studied several schools of Indian philosophy, called darshanas, which cannot be strictly compartmentalized into Hindu and non-Hindu, orthodox and heretical, theist and atheist or idealist and materialist.

Though the early speculations of various schools were unsystematic, later philosophers systematized them through the sutras and commentaries on the sutras (called the *bhashyas*). Various branches of philosophy, such as metaphysics, epistemology, logic and ethics, developed well enough to stand up to any other system of philosophy in the world.

If Indian philosophy were to be revived today, it would have to take into consideration new developments in the west and the east to regain its glory.

Answers

2. Harappan Philosophy: Exploring Ancient Insights and Beliefs

1. B	2. C	3. C	4. C	5. B

3. Philosophy of the Vedas: Tribal and Pastoral Origins

1. B	2. D	3. A	4. B	5. B
6. A	7. A	8. B	9. C	

4. The Philosophy of the Early Upanishads : Path to Knowledge and Salvation

1. B	2. C	3. B	4. C	5. B
6. B	7. D			

5. The Ajivika Philosophy: Determinism Has Its Sway

1. Yes	2. No	3. No	4. No	5. Yes
6. Yes	7. Yes	8. A	9. Yes	

10. Buddhist Philosophy: The Causal Chain

1. No	2. Yes	3. C	4. A	5. Yes
6. Yes	7. No	8. Yes		

11. Jaina Philosophy: Reality Is Manifold

1. C	2. Yes	3. Yes	4. Yes	5. Yes
6. No	7. Yes			

12. Philosophy of the Charvaka (Lokayata): This-Worldly and Materialist

1. Yes	2. No	3. Yes	4. No	5. Yes
6. Yes	7. Yes	8. No		

13. Saankhya and Yoga: Purusha and Prakrit

1. No	2. Yes	3. No	4. No	5. Yes
6. Yes				

14. Nyaya: Rational, Coherent Inquiry

1. C	2. Yes	3. Yes	4. B	5. Yes
6. No	7. Yes			

15. Mimansa: Putting Rituals above God

1. No	2. Yes	3. Yes	4. No	5. Yes
6. A	7. D			

16. Vedanta: The All-Powerful Brahman

1. Yes	2. No	3. Yes	4. No	5. Yes
6. Yes	7. C	8. B	9. No	10. No

17. Bhagavad-Gita: A New Philosophy and Code of Ethics

1. B	2. C	3. C

18. Tantra and Shaktism: Emphasis on Female Principle

1. B	2. C	3. C

19. Ayurveda: Body, Soul and Mind

1. No	2. Yes	3. No	4. Yes

20. Bhakti Movement: Devotion and Love

1. No	2. No	3. No	4. Yes	5. Yes

Acknowledgements

I've long wanted to write a simple introduction to Indian philosophical systems, the *darshanas*, accessible to both lay readers and serious students of philosophy. When Hachette India accepted my proposal, I was thrilled. However, as I began writing, I realized the immense scope of the project. Each Indian philosophical system is complex, with various interpretations and evolving ideas.

In this book, I aim to introduce readers to the fundamental concepts of different philosophical schools and highlight major differences among them, focusing more on the essence of each school rather than delving into intricate details. I've provided explanations for necessary terms and definitions where needed.

I've avoided imposing categories such as astika and nastika, idealist and materialist schools, allowing readers to draw their own conclusions. My narrative is inclusive, covering not only well-known schools but also the philosophies of the medical schools of Sushruta and Charaka, philosophical trends in South India from the Sangam Age to the time of Tiruvalluvar, and the Bhakti movement.

I am deeply indebted to earlier classics on Indian philosophy, especially '*A History of Indian Philosophy*' by Surendranath Dasgupta, and '*Lokayata: A Study in Ancient Indian Materialism*' by Debiprasad Chattopadhyaya. Translations and commentaries by scholars like George Thibaut, John Davies, Rhys Davids, A.L. Basham, and others have been invaluable.

I express my sincere gratitude to all those who have contributed to the publication of this book, particularly to Anirban Sarkar and Arunima Dharanipragada for their endearing engagement and patience.

With only a basic knowledge of classical Sanskrit and Tamil, I have attempted to explore texts and commentaries referred to in this book with the help of translations. I welcome feedback from scholars and readers to help me improve this work.

Raghavan Srinivasan
New Delhi, August 2023

Reading List

Ballantyne, James R. 1885. *The Saankhya Aphorisms of Kapila*, Trubner & Co. London.

Basham, A. L. (2003) 1951. *History and Doctrines of the Ajivikas: A Vanished Religion*. Indian edn. London: Luzac & Co.

Chatterjee, Amita. *Naturalism in Classical Indian Philosophy*, The Stanford Encyclopedia of Philosophy (Winter 2021 Edition), Edward N. Zalta (ed.). URL: <https://plato.stanford.edu/archives/win2021/entries/naturalism-india/>.

Chatterjee, Satischandra and Datta, Dhirendranath. 2007. *An Introduction to Indian Philosophy*. New Delhi: Rupa Publications.

Chattopadhyaya, Debiprasad. (1992). 1959. *Lokayata: A Study in Ancient Indian Materialism*. New Delhi: People's Publishing House.

Dasgupta, Surendranath. 2018. *A History of Indian Philosophy, Volume 1–2*. New Delhi: Rupa Publications.

Davids, Rhys T.W. (Translated from the Pali of the Digha Nikhaya): 1899. *Dialogues of the Buddha*. Vol. I. Delhi: Low Price Publications.

Davids, Rhys. 1907. *Buddhism: Its History and Literature*. New York: G.P. Putnam's Sons.

Davies, John. 1907. *Hindu Philosophy: The Bhagavad Gita or the Sacred Lay*. London: Kegan Paul, Trench, Trubner & Co. Ltd.

Devy, G.N., et al. 2023. *The Indians: Histories of a Civilization*. New Delhi: Aleph Book Company.

Garbe, R. 1895. *The Saankhya Pravachana Bhasya*. Harvard Oriental Series, Vol II. Cambridge.

Hanlon, Julie. 2013. 'Early History of Jainism and Migrations to South India'. *Sramana*, July-September 2013.

Jha, Ganganadha (English translation). 1942. *The Chandogyopanishad with the Commentary of Shankara*. Pune: Oriental Book Agency.

Kaegi, Adolf. 1880. *The Rigveda: The Oldest Literature of the Indians.* Boston.

Karashima, Noboru. 2014. *A Concise History of South India: Issues and Interpretations.* New Delhi: Oxford University Press.

Kingsbury, F. , Phillips. G.E. 1921. *Hymns of the Tamil Saivite Saints.* Oxford University Press. London.

Murugan, Dr. V. (Translated). 2000. *Tolkappiyam*. Chennai: Institute of Asian Studies.

Olivelle, Patrick. 1998. *The Early Upanisads Annotated Text And Translation*. New York: Oxfor University Press.

Singh, Upinder. 2009. *A History of Ancient and Early Medieval India.* Delhi: Pearson.

Tagore, Rabindranath (Translation with the assistance of Evelyn Underhill). 1915. *Songs of Kabir*. New York: The Macmillan Company

Thapar, Romila. 2002. *Early India: From the Origins to AD 1300.* Gurugram: Penguin Books.

Thibaut, George (Translated). 1890. *The Vedanta-Sutras with the Commentary By Sankara*. Oxford: Clarendon Press.

Vidyabhusana, Satish Chandra. (Translated by). 1913. *The Sacred Books of The Hindus, Vol. VIII, The Nyaya Sutras of Gotama.* Prayagraj: Panini Office

Zvelebil, Kamil V. 1974. *Tamil Literature, A History of Indian Literature, Volume X.* Wiesbaden: Otto Harrassowitz.

Index

V

Y

Attribution for Images

Figure 1: Page 5—CCA-SA 3.0 Unported. https://commons.wikimedia.org/wiki/File:Picture_of_original_Godess.jpg

Figure 2: Page 20—CCA-SA 4.0 International. https://commons.wikimedia.org/wiki/File:Chandogya_Upanishad_sample_ii,_Samaveda,_Sanskrit,_Devanagari_script,_1865_CE_manuscript.jpg

Figure 3: Page 26—CC0 1.0 Universal. https://commons.wikimedia.org/wiki/File:Ajivika_Monk_in_a_Gandhara_sculpture_of_the_Mahaparinirvana.jpg

Figure 4: Page 30—AnilD/Shutterstock.com

Figure 5: Page 46—CCA 4.0 International. https://commons.wikimedia.org/wiki/File:Eight_Patriarchs_of_the_Shingon_Sect_of_Buddhism_Nagarjuna_Cropped.jpg

Figure 7: Page 65—CCA-SA 2.0 Generic. https://commons.wikimedia.org/w/index.php?curid=59461928

Figure 16: Page 161—YASH DINESHBHAI PATEL/Shutterstock.com

Chapter opener icons (pages 1, 3, 8, 16, 26, 37, 58, 73, 85, 105, 122, 135, 155, 159, 167, 176): flaticon.com. These pages have been designed using assets from flaticon.com

Notes

1. Exploring the Depths of Indian Philosophical Insight

[1]Epistemology is the branch of philosophy that pertains to the study of knowledge, belief and the nature of truth.

[2]Logic in philosophy deals with the principles of valid reasoning and the systematic study of inference and argumentation.

[3]Ethics in philosophy concerns moral principles, values and judgments regarding what is right and wrong in human conduct.

[4]Aesthetics in philosophy explores the nature of beauty, art, perception and the philosophy of art and beauty.

[5]Political philosophy enquires into the nature of political institutions, governance, justice, rights, and the ideal organization of societies.

[6]Axiology in philosophy deals with the study of values, including ethics, aesthetics and the philosophy of human values.

3. The Vedas: Tribal and Pastoral Origins

[1]*The Ridveda*, Kaegi, p. 89

[2]Ibid., p.90

4. The Early Upanishads: Path to Knowledge and Salvation

[1]Dasgupta, S. *A History of Indian Philosophy*, Vol. 1. p. 31

[2]Singh, Upinder. *A History of Ancient and Early Medieval India*. pp. 202–204

5. Ajivika: Determinism has its Sway

[1]The Lokayata school of philosophy was a materialistic atheistic school in ancient India that emphasized empirical observation and denied the existence of souls or the afterlife.

[2]Chattopadhyaya, Debiprasad, *Lokayata*, pp. 518–19

[3]Ibid., pp. 523–4

6. Buddha: The Causal Chain

[1]Dasgupta, S. *A History of Indian Philosophy*, Vol. 1. pp. 109–11

7. Jain: Reality is Manifold

[1]Dasgupta, S. *A History of Indian Philosophy*, Vol. 1. pp. 175–76

8. Charvaka (Lokayata): This-worldly and Materialist

[1]Dasgupta, S. *A History of Indian Philosophy*, Vol. 1. pp. 783–84

[2]Chattopadhyaya, Debiprasad quoting Rhys Davids, *Lokayata*, p. 22

[3]Ibid. p. 22

9. Saankhya and Yoga: Purusha and Prakriti

[1]Chatterjee, S, Datta D. *An Introduction to Indian Philosophy*. pp. 238–39

[2]Garbe, R. *Saankhya Pravacan Bhasya*. p. 365

[3]Chattopadhyaya, D. *Lokayata*. pp. 364–372

12. Vedanta: The All-Powerful Brahman

[1]Dasgupta, S. *A History of Indian Philosophy*, Vol. 1. pp. 430–433

13. Bhagavat Gita: A New Philosophy and Code of Ethics

[1]Davies, J (translated by). *The Bhagavad Gita*.

14. Tantra and Shaktism: Emphasis on the Female Principle

[1]Singh, Upinder. *A History of Ancient and Early Medieval India*. p. 511

[2]Thapar, R. *History of Early India*. pp. 485–86

[3]Chattopadhyay, *Lokayata*, pp. 272–73

[4]Ibid. p. 264

[5]Ibid. p. 232

[6]Ibid. p. 245

[7]Singh, Upinder. *A History of Ancient and Early Medieval India*. pp. 439–40

[8]Chattopadhyaya, Debiprasad. *Lokayata*. pp. 359–364

15. Ayurveda: Body, Soul and Mind

[1]Samhita is a methodological collection of texts or verses

[2]Dasgupta, S. *A History of Indian Philosophy*, Vol. 2. pp. 1–6

[3]Chattopadhyaya, Debiprasad. *Lokayata*. p. 368

16. The Bhakti Movement: Devotion and Love

[1]Thapar, Romila. *Early India: From the Origins to AD 1300*. pp. 350–355